PAUL RIMMASCH

FINGER PRINTS

AND PHAN TOMS

True Tales
of Law
Enforcement
Encounters
with the
Paranormal
and the
Strange

Schiffer Publishing Ltd

4880 Lower Valley Road • Atglen, PA 19310

Designed by Matt Goodman
Type set in Tungsten and Trade Gothic

ISBN: 978-0-7643-5529-5
Printed in the United Sates of America

Published by Schiffer Publishing, Ltd.
4880 Lower Valley Road
Atglen, PA 19310
Phone: (610) 593-1777; Fax: (610) 593-2002
E-mail: Info@schifferbooks.com
Web: www.schifferbooks.com

For our complete selection of fine books on this and related subjects, please visit our website at www.schifferbooks.com. You may also write for a free catalog.

Schiffer Publishing's titles are available at special discounts for bulk purchases for sales promotions or premiums. Special editions, including personalized covers, corporate imprints, and excerpts, can be created in large quantities for special needs. For more information, contact the publisher.

We are always looking for people to write books on new and related subjects. If you have an idea for a book, please contact us at proposals@schifferbooks.com.

To my wife Jessie.
This book is just one of your many great ideas.

In Loving Memory of
"The Dude"
March 4, 2004–September 6, 2015

Contents

Foreword

This selection of stories, collected by the author from various law enforcement officers, ranges from the eerie to the amusing, through the tender to the thought-provoking. If you enjoy a tale well told, if you can believe in something incredible, if you can conjure the leisure of time in these busy days to sit and peruse these pages, then this collection will not disappoint.

When my good friend, Paul, asked me to edit this anthology, I was piqued. I personally have little experience with the paranormal unless it is amusing on screen, but these stories remind me there is much in this world of which we know little. I submit to you the dogs of southeastern Los Angeles, the mysterious patient, and a lost cell phone, among others.

This compilation is more than a simple set of ghost stories. The author's lighthearted insights into and experiences in the world of crime scene investigation make this read doubly fascinating. He is a sort of James Herriot of the CSI world.

I sincerely hope you enjoy these reminiscences and reports. They make few claims, but they offer their evidences boldly, and sometimes they poke fun at themselves. They might even make a believer out of you.

Reader, Beware.
Crystine L. Riches

Acknowledgments

Thanks to everyone who ever strapped on their gun and badge, or their camera and fingerprint brush, and rode out into a dark and stormy night.

Special thanks to my friend, Katy; you kept this project going whenever it stalled.

Introduction

What do the topics of fingerprints and law enforcement have in common with phantoms and the paranormal? Ostensibly, nothing. Forensic science and law enforcement deal with facts and proof. As the old saying in our business goes, "It's not what you know. It's what you can prove." On the other hand, the paranormal deals with unanswered questions and improvable anecdotes from dark and stormy nights and lonely roads. How can these two seemingly contradictory topics coexist peacefully in one book?

I did not start out writing this book for any reason other than the fact that I love a good story and good storytelling. "What does that have to do with the topics at hand?" you may ask. Everything. There is plenty of downtime in police work. "Hurry up and wait" is the rule rather than the exception. Police shows on television never show cops waiting for two hours for a search warrant to be signed by a judge, but that is reality. When one is waiting endlessly outside a house for a standoff to resolve there is not much to do. I mean, it is not like you can read a book or watch a movie with the news cameras pointed at you, right? Swapping stories is one of the few ways to pass the time, so the storytelling culture is alive and well in law enforcement. This form of camaraderie is one of the things people love about this line of work. It is something they very much miss when they retire.

In my nearly two decades of being involved in this glorious exchange of ideas, the ghostly and bizarre stories have been my favorite. This book is a compendium of some of those wonderful yarns and my homage to the brave men and women who shared them with me. Be that as it may, I realize this subject matter may open myself to ridicule. "How could a supposed man of science deal with such an unconventional topic?" one might ask. That is a good question. When I think about how to respond, my thoughts return to a recurring experience that unfortunately I have had all too often during my last twenty years on the job.

Imagine you are standing in the middle of a street and it is nighttime. It is dark—pitch dark. The only light available to you is the beam from the flashlight in your hand and the flickering colored lights of emergency vehicles. Not only is it dark, it is cold, too. The bitter wind knifes through your clothing and bites at your flesh, mocking your apparel's meager attempt to keep it out. At your feet, crumpled on the merciless asphalt, are the remains of a young person whose light was extinguished way before its time. The sobs of a grieving mother and father may be within earshot, or they may only be in your imagination.

At times like this the world of sterile labs, university classrooms, and peer-reviewed scientific journals is far, far away. A fleet of disdainful academicians can't prevent you from looking down at the broken body before you and having the uncanny feeling that some essence of that person remains. A gaggle of skeptics cannot dissuade you from occasionally asking that essence a question or two in your mind, the practice of which carries its own set of dangers (see chapter three). Call it foolishness, call it sentiment, but until you have been on that dark street, standing over a similar tragedy, you might want to hold off on passing judgment, especially since I am not alone in my interest in the subject.

When I started asking around at work to see if any other investigators or officers had stories for me, I wondered if such inquires would be met with scorn; they were not. In fact, many officers seemed relieved that they finally had a safe outlet to share some of their creepy experiences. Such an interest in and a willingness to share stories of the paranormal is not just a northern Utah thing. When I was a guest on the nationally syndicated radio talk show *Coast to Coast AM* with George Noory for an unrelated writing endeavor, the subject of police-related ghost stories was brought up. During the call-in portion of the show, cops from all across the country contacted us with their own spooky tales. This experience showed me that my interest in this subject was by no means an aberration.

So yes, to answer the original question: I do think the topics of crime scene investigation and ghosts belong together. Do we not walk with death on nearly a daily basis? Are we—the supposed unbiased finders of fact—intellectually flexible enough to admit we do not know everything? Is not what happens to us after death—the ultimate mystery—worthy of a group of mystery solvers to examine?

That is quite enough pontificating for now. May I now address a few housekeeping items before you proceed with this book? First, there are many theories circulating about what a ghost or haunting actually is. Some researchers take the conventional stance that a ghost is the spirit of a departed individual. Others make the claim that a haunting is just an echo in time. This book does not make any attempt to bolster one argument or another; it is a collection of stories. Nevertheless, in compiling these tales, I did notice some interesting patterns. You be the judge.

Second, as much as this work is not a treatise on the scientific nature of hauntings, it is also not a book of true crime. I am deliberately vague about the details regarding the crimes related to the presented stories. This is partially out of stylistic concern. I wanted this book to be more about the awe and wonder of the story and not about the gory details. Think "sitting around the campfire as a kid," not an episode of *48 Hours* or *Dateline*. More importantly, I omitted details out of respect for the victims and their families. They have suffered enough and do not need to have their names pulled back into the media. I hope and pray that they have found some peace.

I will add that tragedies have the bad habit of repeating themselves over and over again and following similar patterns. If for some reason you assume you know which event I am referencing, don't. Unfortunately, events similar to those described herein happen all too frequently.

So there you have it. Dim the lights, pull up a comfy chair, wrap yourself in a warm blanket, and enjoy this little anthology. Oh, and don't forget: if you hear something go bump in the night, it may not be a burglar.

Chapter One
The Answered Plea

I have a love-hate relationship with crime scenes where a firearm was used. On the one hand, gun crimes have the potential to generate an enormous amount of useful evidence. Bullets, bullet fragments, and shell casings may be matched back to the gun that fired them. If the gun was the kind that ejects casings, the positions of the shell casings on the ground can give you a general idea of where the person who shot the gun was standing when the shots were fired. Perhaps best of all are instances where the bullet or bullets entered one side of a stationary object and exited out of the other side. With such "through and through" scenarios, a trajectory rod or laser can be used to determine exactly where the shot came from and give you a good idea of where it is going. Such evidence is extremely important in crime scene reconstruction and evidence recovery.

On the other hand, such an abundance of evidence often equates to an equal amount of frustration. In cases where there are multiple shooters, such as an officer-involved shooting or a gang shoot-out, there may be dozens if not hundreds of rounds fired. This makes for days, if not weeks, of painstaking effort trying to figure out who shot what and from where.

Furthermore, shell casings are relatively easy to find in a parking lot during the middle of the day, but put those same shell casings in deep grass or in a wooded area at night and you have sleepless nights, sore backs, and spent flashlight batteries.

Needless to say, if you are working a case where some guy pops off two rounds in his kitchen and you find the casings on the middle of the floor and the slugs lodged in the door of the fridge, you are loving life. If you have a running gun battle with automatic rifles covering twenty city blocks which mirrors a scene from a "Die Hard" movie . . . you wish you had chosen a different career path.

Most shooting scenes are somewhere in between. And so it was with a case where a man gunned down his estranged wife and her mother after he had taken them hostage and bound them. It was a nasty, extremely personal affair as a crime. As a crime scene it was fairly straightforward, and for the most part was contained to one room, even though dozens of rounds had been fired.

That being said, every crime scene possesses its share of challenges and nuances, so one might forgive a young crime scene investigator for taking a somewhat novel approach in his attempt to put it all together. You see, based on the ebb and flow of crime scene activities, you may find yourself all alone in the room with someone who has died a violent and bloody death, even though you are working with a full crew.

On such an occasion, my colleague Mitch found himself all alone, on one knee in front of the younger of the two victims, seeking to fully understand and reconstruct the chain of events that had led to her death. In what may be described as a purely mental exercise, he audibly said to the woman, "Talk to me. Help us figure out what happened to you."

I think it is safe to say that Mitch was not necessarily expecting an answer. I think it is even safer to say that he certainly did not expect every light in the house to suddenly go out—which is exactly what happened. So there Mitch was, alone in complete darkness with two victims of a horribly violent crime. To make matters worse, Mitch was seized with a feeling of complete and utter dread. Now, one might respond that this sensation was caused by the unnatural and awkward situation Mitch found himself in at that moment.

While there may be some validity to that argument, any person arguing that point was not the one standing there in the dark with two corpses. Mitch certainly maintains that his feelings were well beyond the shock of the situation. To this day he can't fully explain exactly what he was feeling, but it shook him to the very core.

After what seemed like an eternity to Mitch the lights popped back on. In reality, they were probably only out for thirty seconds to a minute, but that was enough for him. Leaving the scene, Mitch went outside to the staging area to find a little company. He expected to find the rest of us talking about the brief and unexpected power outage . . . but we weren't.

The conversation went something like this, "Did you guys notice the power going out?" said Mitch.

"What are you talking about?" the rest of us replied.

"I was in the house . . . the lights went out. Didn't you see it?"

"No. We were standing out here the whole time. We didn't see any lights go out."

"Come on, guys, stop messing around. I was standing there in pitch black," implored Mitch, suspecting a joke.

"Mitch, we're telling you," we responded, "Neither the outside lights of this house nor any of the other lights on this street went out!"

Well that, as they say, was that. Mitch was left with an unsettled feeling in the pit of his stomach. Fortunately for him, the demands of a double homicide scene did not give Mitch a lot of time to dwell on the odd occurrence. He quickly shook the whole thing off and got back to work. After processing the scene we all went home and things got back to normal, or as close to normal as a crime scene investigator can approximate. For Mitch, the mystery of the lights faded farther and farther in the rearview mirror. Whatever had happened—whatever he had felt—was all behind him . . . right?

If you wake up one morning and your alarm clock is blinking 12:00, signifying an interruption in power, but nothing else in the house show signs of such an interruption, you could probably explain that away as a problem with the clock. If every light and plug in a certain room cease to function one minute and then are fine another, you might blame the newness of the house. If lights all over the house go on and off randomly, you could easily blame faulty light bulbs.

If any one of these strange occurrences happened to any rational person they could explain them away. But if every one of these things happens with increasing regularity a person begins to take notice, and Mitch did begin to take notice. To make matters worse, Mitch would often have the strong, palpable, undeniable sensation that he was not alone . . . even when he most certainly was. This was especially disconcerting when that sensation woke him up in the middle of the night!

And then there was "the Dude." The Dude is a dog: a pug, to be exact. Although pugs are known as an eccentric breed, in the days and weeks after this homicide, the Dude began to act very strangely indeed. Sometimes he would appear to be watching someone or something walking back and forth in a completely empty room. His eyes and head moved slowly back and forth, but nothing was there. Other times he stared up at the ceiling, issuing low growls. Then, for no reason Mitch could discern, the upstairs toilet became an object of intense interest for the Dude. He would stand by it and bark for extended periods of time.

All of these bizarre occurrences and peculiar canine behavior had Mitch at his wits end. Being a man of science and learning, Mitch probably would have never wrapped his mind around all of this had fate not intervened on his behalf. A young lady visited Mitch's home one day who was a medium of sorts. For her, the veil between this world and the next is very thin. Based on her own impressions, and upon observing the mercurial conduct of the Dude, she concluded that a ghost had followed Mitch home from a crime scene. After questioning Mitch about his recent cases, she concluded that it was the spirit of the young woman he had asked for help who was plaguing him.

Mitch's intuitive friend explained to him that the act of asking the dead woman for help had opened an ethereal door of sorts. She, having been rejected in the most severe way possible, had sought someone who needed her and had latched on to him and followed him home.

Perhaps all of this was a bunch of new age mumbo jumbo, but this revelation made Mitch feel better. It gave him a modicum of understanding, and more importantly, sympathy for this poor departed woman and her plight. It also seemed to make the restless spirit feel better, because the frequency of the strange events in Mitch's house were lessened, and he was not particularly bothered when something odd did happen. The only thing that continued to vex Mitch was his dog's continued affinity for the upstairs toilet.

Although this episode turned out well enough for Mitch, the rest of us working in law enforcement are left with a nagging question: "Who exactly have we brought home to dinner?"

Chapter Two
The Parked Cop

 Those of us engaged in law enforcement fieldwork do not get to take breaks like people working in other occupations generally do. Say, for example, you work retail. When your break time comes, you leave the sales floor and go into a break room. Be it palatial or dingy, it is a magical place where you can sit down and relax, get a bite to eat, make a call or two, or even watch a little television, all blessedly well away from customers and their questions and concerns. Similar scenarios are played out in many workplaces across the world, whether it is an office building or an auto shop.

Such is not the case for people in uniform. If—and that is a big "if"—your call volume has slowed down enough that you attempt to take a break, your best bet is to try and grab a quick drink or snack (yes, donuts are a favorite) from a gas station or a convenience store. The trouble is, whether you are standing in the parking lot or waiting in line, the citizens of your jurisdiction view this as a perfect time to have a chat.

Sometimes people want to complain about how they were treated by other law enforcement officers, or have a discussion about the finer points of the law. Other times directions to this place or that are required, or a fix-it ticket* needs to be signed.

---

* A fix-it ticket is a conditional citation given by an officer who sees something wrong with your car. If you get the problem fixed in a given amount of time and demonstrate it to another officer, they will sign the fix-it ticket and a fine will not be levied.

Oftentimes, one is accosted by persons under the influence of their favorite substances—legal or otherwise. And many times people want to give things they have found to you. I personally have been handed literally everything from drug paraphernalia to a baby owl while standing in the parking lot of my favorite 7-Eleven.

Hopefully this last paragraph does not come across like I am complaining too much, because much of this parking lot-based interaction is very positive. Many people just stop to tell you they appreciate your service or tell you to "be safe." Sometimes veterans or retired cops sense a kindred spirit (no pun intended) and stop by to swap stories.

Be that as it may, it is at times difficult to catch your breath and rest for a minute. To make matters worse, since most officers now have laptops in their cars for the express purpose of writing reports, it is hard to catch up on one's paperwork with such constant interruptions, be they pleasant or otherwise.

The above-mentioned paradigm often necessitates that officers find a secluded spot where they—out of the view of the public—can relax or tend to their clerical duties. It should also be noted that in some jurisdictions shifts can be so slow that an officer will find such a spot and park because there is literally nothing to do. This occurs mostly in rural areas or during the winter months.

It should come as no surprise that many of the ghostly stories I have heard over the years revolve around the penchant of officers to seek out lonely spots. It is also safe to say that only people who have a handgun strapped to their hip and a shotgun mounted behind the seat would park alone at night in some of these locations.

Such was the case with a deputy named Mike. Mike was pulling a graveyard shift in a rural area of Weber County on a cold, clear northern Utah winter night. The police radio lay completely and utterly silent: no calls for service dispatched and no radio chatter among fellow officers. I have experienced such nights myself, with the radio so quiet I find myself checking it periodically to make sure it has not been accidentally turned off.

So it was with Mike. Having patrolled his area multiple times and found all well, he decided to pass some time at a secluded locality named Cemetery Point. It is important to note that Cemetery Point is not one of those euphemistic names people give places, such as a shopping mall and its accompanying enormous parking lot christened "The Meadows" or the like;

there is actually a cemetery at Cemetery Point, and Mike was parked right in the middle of it. Did I mention it was the middle of the night? Certainly no one would bother him there, or so he thought.

As Mike checked his computer, he suddenly felt an extremely unnerving sensation. Somewhere out there in the dark, a pair of unseen eyes suddenly fixed upon him. For someone who has never experienced this sensation it may be hard to imagine, but there are times when one absolutely knows one is being watched, even if no spectator is apparent. You just know it in your bones. Mike knew it.

He slammed the screen of his laptop down and instinctively moved his hand closer to his side arm. Heart pounding in his chest, Mike scanned the gloom surrounding his truck, seeking the owner of those eyes that he still so keenly felt boring into him. Was it a friend or foe? Cops are notorious practical jokers. It would not have been out of the question for another officer to have been trying to sneak up on Mike and scare him. Could it have been a large animal, or something else entirely? As his eyes struggled to shake the influence of the luminous laptop screen and adjust to the darkness around him, Mike looked toward the front of the vehicle. What he saw caused him to instantly pop his truck into drive and take off. You see, although it was a still, fogless night, Mike clearly witnessed a shapeless yet distinct formation of mist rise up from one side of his truck, flow slowly across the hood, and then disappear into the night.

Of course, one could argue that it would not be unheard of for a random patch of fog to appear on a frigid, wintry night such as the one in question. And although such may be the case, if you combine one set of unseen eyes and one small cloud that appears seemingly out of nowhere in the middle of the night in a deserted county cemetery, you may get what we have in this instance: a deputy who did not look in the rearview mirror as he left Cemetery Point behind him.

Another time and another place finds a solitude-seeking officer of the law not struggling against the cold of the high mountains but rather the languor of a warm ocean breeze. You see, John was patrolling a rural area of Massachusetts very near the coast. Although it was the height of summer—a time particularly busy for law enforcement—this night was extremely quiet: no radio traffic, no calls for service, no nothing.

After patrolling his area multiple times, checking the things he was supposed to check, and doing the things he was supposed to do, John found himself staring four o'clock in the morning squarely in the face with nothing to do. At this point, John decided to do what we have established officers do in cases like this: he sought a secluded spot. The spot John found was well suited for his purposes: a dead-end street far away from any houses whose sides were overgrown with tall reeds and sea grasses. He backed his car down to the end of this street to a point where the foliage virtually engulfed his patrol car, rolled his window down, and settled in, intent on waiting out the rest of his shift.

Anyone who has worked a graveyard shift knows that it is the last few hours before dawn that challenge the resolve to stay awake the most. Furthermore, there are very few things more soothing to the senses than a balmy ocean breeze and its faint hint of brine. Add to this mix the gentle rustling of the reeds in said breeze, and I hope the reader will forgive Officer John if his eyelids began to grow very heavy indeed. Fight it as he may, the delicious night air, the dim lights of his dashboard, and the soothing music of the night eventually overcame our intrepid officer, and he slipped into the realm of consciousness between wakefulness and sleep known as the *hypnagogic* state commonly called twilight.

As we all know, this twilight state can be a tricky thing. It is sometimes difficult to differentiate between the dreams that are coming and the reality that is going. That being said, one could argue that Officer John did not actually hear what he thought he heard at the moment he slipped from awareness. You see, to this day, John claims he plainly heard in the reeds just feet from his open squad car window a young boy and a young girl . . . giggling.

Still half asleep, John's senses literally screamed at him. He did not know why, but his mind ordered him to flee from that place not when he got around to it . . . but now, right that very moment. As he slammed the car into "drive" and roared out of the area there was no internal discussion on the unpredictability of perception in the hypnagogic state, nor any rationalization regarding flesh-and-blood children playing in a deserted patch of weeds at four o'clock in the morning. There was only an emphatic subconscious warning and screeching rubber.

Another curious tale comes from the cemetery not far from where this book was written. The Ogden City Cemetery is old by western US standards and is a storied resting place with an eclectic list of residents. You can find founding members of the Mormon Church, the inventor of the Browning automatic rifle, the voice of the Magic Mirror in the original *Snow White and the Seven Dwarfs*, and almost everyone in between resting beneath its tree-lined lanes and ornate tombstones.

By city ordinance, the cemetery closes at dark. This fact brings cops to its dark and secluded streets for two reasons: one, they patrol the cemetery to keep trespassers out; and two, when they accomplish their first objective, it makes an ideal location for officers to take a break or catch up on paperwork.

Most, if not all, old cemeteries have ghost stories of one sort or another attached to them. The Ogden City Cemetery is certainly no different. Ghostly yarns from this hallowed ground range from your garden-variety spooks to a fantastical account regarding a statue of a World War I soldier whose head supposedly swivels to follow the cars that circle his platform the requisite number of times. The most enduring paranormal resident of the Ogden City Cemetery is a restive spirit named Flo.

Flo, or Florence Louise Grange as she was known in life, was struck down in the springtime of her life by the Spanish Flu. When the beautiful and athletic fifteen-year-old passed away in 1918, it broke the hearts of her family and friends.

Sometime after her death—no one remembers exactly when—the story began to circulate that motorists who drove to her gravestone at night and flashed their headlights three times would see Flo's restless spirit materialize right before their very eyes. The fact that her appearance is tied to the activity of automobiles has fostered tales that she was run over by a car, or that she is a jilted lover still waiting for her unfaithful boyfriend to pick her up. Although these archetypal urban legends could explain Flo's affinity for headlights, they do not apply to this young girl who passed peacefully from this life one cold winter's day long ago. There is no easy explanation for why she appears in the manner that she does.

It is not the search for the answer to this esoteric question that has caused generations of thrill seekers to sneak into the Ogden City Cemetery after dark, but rather, the chance to see the famous apparition. People from all over the region were acquainted with Flo's antics even before the age of the internet, and seeking her out is almost a rite of passage for adventurous youth.

Oddly enough, people leave coins, trinkets, candles, and religious ornaments on her grave, perhaps in an effort to provoke an appearance. When Flo appears—and there are countless examples of her doing so—she takes the form of a girl, a glowing orb, or every now and then a creeping illuminated mist. And sometimes, as a few officers have found out, she will even appear unbidden.

This brings us to another dark and lonely night and another officer trying to catch up on his reports. As I mentioned before, the grand old cemetery at the center of Ogden is a preferred location to do just that. On this particular night, our officer friend looked up from his computer and something caught his eye. Parked at the back of the cemetery, he saw a distinct blue mist hovering over the gravestones. This officer blinked hard and rubbed his eyes. Were his eyes playing tricks on him? Nope . . . the mist was still there. He observed it for a while; it seemed to be slinking closer to his location. There was nothing to account for the oddity. There were no cars or streetlights nearby that could be casting this eerie glow. It was a moonless night, and stars are not bright enough to cause the anomaly. It was not too long before the blue glow melted away. Observing this, the unflappable officer shrugged and went about his business.

When he told me this story, I offered that he had a run in with the famous Flo. He concurred that the incident did fit the pattern of many reported accounts. When I asked him if he was scared by this encounter his response took me off guard. He simply responded, "No. I don't believe in ghosts."

Perhaps it is too easy to explain away a cloud of mist—blue or otherwise—but another officer had an experience that was not as easy to rationalize. One night, an officer named Larry backed his patrol car down a cemetery street very near Flo's final resting place and busied himself with his computer. At one point, he glanced up from his work and saw something that made him do a double take. Floating twenty feet in front of his car was the form of a girl. It slowly crossed the road, stopped above Flo's grave, and then vanished, but not before turning its head and looking right at the startled officer. If this was not unnerving enough for Larry, several dormant candles at the base of the tombstone abruptly sprang to life.

Knowing that sometimes the best tactical decision is to retreat, Larry left the cemetery in haste and did not return for quite some time. He did eventually go back, because the Ogden City Cemetery is just that perfect a place for so many things. He has not seen Flo since, but I am almost certain he is more careful where he points his headlights.

Chapter Three
Who You Gonna Call?

To say that I have been in a few surrealistic situations in my career would certainly be an understatement. In fact, there may not be a more surreal profession in the entire world than law enforcement. Much of it involves being in a scene of graphic violence and not being particularly shaken up by it.

I think of one example where two of my comrades and I paused what we were doing to watch the scene from *Butch Cassidy and the Sundance Kid* where the two heroes make their famous jump into the river. What is so bizarre about three co-workers casually watching a bit of television, you may ask? Well, there was an unfortunate soul at our feet who had been stomped to death and the big screen television we were watching was covered with his blood; it was a very nice cast-off pattern, if I remember correctly.

If you step back and analyze the situation for what it was, it is just plain wrong. I can accept that. Situations like that are a dime a dozen in this business. That is just the way it is.

Needless to say, a good sense of humor is just as important to a person working in law enforcement as a gun and handcuffs are to a patrol officer and the camera and fingerprint kit are to a crime scene investigator. Not only does laughing and joking help render labor less burdensome, as it does in any line of work, but it can be a shield from the psychological trauma inherent in police work—a defense mechanism, if you will.

It is a defense mechanism ill understood by outsiders. If members of the general public saw police officers and crime scene investigators standing in the midst of death and destruction, laughing about an episode of the Simpsons or razzing each other about last night's football game, they would probably be horrified. Be that as it may, when it comes right down to it, it is just another day at the office.

Humor can also be a valuable tool when dealing with the public. I was once told a story about a group of officers who kept getting called to the same house over and over again to investigate complaints about—of all things—ghosts. I hope that this book has established that cops, by and large, have no problem believing in ghosts. In this case, the officers felt the elderly woman in question was plagued more by mental illness than by spirits. Time after time they responded, checked the house, and found nothing, and time after time they left with nothing resolved.

While dealing with people who have the same problem over and over again is commonplace for officers, it can lead to a sense of helplessness, especially when the person is otherwise decent. So it was in this case. What could be done to help this woman?

The answer to that question came one day when the officers found themselves dispatched once again to the now familiar address. For the umpteenth time, the reason for the call was ghosts. When the story was recounted to me, none of the officers involved personally took credit for the game-changing innovation, but when they got to the house, one of them suggested that they take their portable radar guns inside. When the trigger on these traffic monitoring devices is pulled a loud beeping sound issues from the apparatus.

After listening intently to the complainant describe her all-too-familiar problems, the officers assured her that this was her lucky day. They had brought with them their new "ghostbusting" guns, and they told her this new tool would solve her problem once and for all. The officers then commenced going room the room and "firing" their radar guns every few steps, filling the residence with the sound of their desperate plan.

She never called the police again.

Chapter Four
The Fifth Floor

The average person works in an office, a store, or a factory, and keeps relatively regular hours. They leave their places of employment at lunchtime if they leave at all during work hours. The average person seems to have a hard time fathoming the variability and flexibility of a law enforcement work day.

There are shifts that are so busy that an officer does not get a bathroom break, let alone lunch. Then, too, there are times when nothing is going on at all. Investigators need to be on duty in case something does happen, but since calls for service can't be manufactured, one must simply wait for something to happen. Add to this the fact that in law enforcement your jurisdiction is your office—whether a city, county, or state—so if you are in your jurisdiction and ready for a call, you are working.

Private citizens often do not understand this work schedule. This lack of understanding often expresses itself in the form of snarky comments made to officers and crime scene investigators violating what people consider proper work protocol. For example, you could have just finished working thirty-six hours straight processing a grizzly homicide scene. It is eight o'clock in the morning and you need to unwind a bit before you try to get some sleep. I use the word "try" deliberately, because there is such a thing as being too tired to fall asleep.

Anyway, you need to unwind, so you swing by your favorite 7-Eleven to grab a bite to eat and to shoot the breeze with some co-workers. In walks a guy wearing a business suit on his way to work. He views the world as a nine-to-five kind of place. He sees you there, eating a donut and having a laugh with your comrades at eight in the morning and assumes you have gotten an early start on goofing off. Next follows a comment along the lines of, "A little early for a break, isn't it boys?" or, "Boy! I wish I had your job," or the ever popular, "My tax dollars at work, huh?"

Then there are the times you need to run to a store during your shift to buy something you need for work. Say you run into a Home Depot to purchase some plastic sheeting and duct tape for the construction of a makeshift tent for the purpose of processing an entire car for fingerprints using super glue fuming. You are there on official business, with the office credit card in your pocket, but just because you are standing in line, in uniform, at a place most people go on their leisure time, they assume that the stuff in your arms is for a "honey do" and not for work. Again flow the comments—"Working hard or hardly workin'?" is an old standby. Pretty much any time you are seen in public in uniform without a camera or a fingerprint brush in your hands you are susceptible to dirty looks or sarcasm.

There are exceptions to every rule. There is one time of year when being out and about in uniform does not necessarily garner the usual reaction, and that time of year is Halloween. In fact, sometimes people do not even believe you are who you say you are. Such was the case one year when a colleague and I had a call at one of the most haunted places in town—the Ben Lomond Hotel.

Before I go on with my story, I just have to say that the Ben Lomond Hotel is the real deal. Whole books could be written about this place alone, there are that many stories. A typical Ben Lomond Hotel ghost story was told to me one night by a security guard who used to work there. I got to know him one night when I responded to a call at another large hotel in town.

A bunch of drunk guys had run down the halls smashing light fixtures, tipping over potted plants, and generally spreading hate and discontent. A heck of a way to spend the night before Thanksgiving, isn't it? Anyway, I was to photograph the damage, and this security guard was to accompany me and make sure I got to all the areas I needed to go.

As we walked along and chatted he revealed to me that he had once worked at the Ben Lomond. When I asked him if he had ever seen anything ghostly there he got a little quiet and gave some evasive answer. I figured that he had probably caught some grief from his buddies about things he had told them, so I tried to reassure him by telling him flat out that I was a believer and would not give him any guff. This straightforward approach seemed to work, and he opened up and told me one of the creepiest stories I had ever heard.

One night, as he was making his rounds, he found himself walking across the grand lobby of the Ben Lomond Hotel. In the still of the early morning hours his footsteps echoed hypnotically on the marble floor in the vast open hall, lulling his mind to a state of ease. At this time of day one did not expect to see many guests out and about. This was the easy part of his job. He just had to make sure there was no trouble and did not have to interact with the public.

When he rounded a corner, something unexpected jarred him out of his tranquility. Walking right toward him was an elderly woman. He told me there was nothing extremely peculiar about her other than a strange, far-away look in her eyes. It was like she did not even see him. So taken aback was he by her sudden appearance that he forgot his manners and failed to address her as she breezed past him.

The woman also seemed to have disregarded the characteristic courtesy of her generation, for she did not so much as give him a glance. He quickly came to his senses and realized that professional courtesy mandated that he see if she required assistance, especially at such a late hour. The trouble was, when he spun around to ask, she was gone. The mystery guest was nowhere to be seen. No sound of footsteps marked her passing. To reiterate, the Ben Lomond Hotel is the real deal.

My co-worker Sandy and I found ourselves in the parking lot of the Ben Lomond the night before Halloween. It was Saturday night, and people were getting a jump on the parties. A fight in the bar attached to the hotel had spilled outside, and the crime scene investigators had been called to the scene to photograph the injuries sustained by the belligerents. It was a quick job, and we soon were standing there, staring up at one of the tallest buildings in Ogden.

"This place is haunted, you know," I said, matter-of-factly.

"Really?" replied Sandy.

"Yup."

"Oh, come on."

"You'll see," I returned. "Let's go in and talk to the person at the front desk."

Having no other calls pending, Sandy agreed to go in and chat up the clerk. After entering the grand doors and climbing a short flight of marble stairs we reached the front desk. The clerk, seeing two people in uniform walk up to her and knowing what had just transpired in the parking lot, certainly expected some sort of official business. I am not sure if she was relieved or annoyed when we started asking her about ghosts. Her carefully crafted façade of customer service did not belie what her true feelings might be.

As we conversed with the hotel employee, a large group of drunken revelers, all in costume, poured through the door that connected the bar with the hotel. Soon the lobby was teeming with fairies, devils, and disco kings—you name it. There was even a "John Stockton" equipped with shorty-shorts. It was not long before one of the male partygoers spotted us. He sauntered over, leaned luxuriously against the antique woodwork of the counter, cocked his head to one side, and asked mockingly, "What are you guys supposed to be?"

Both Sandy and I responded slowly, "We're crime scene investigators." The dynamics of this awkward situation had not yet dawned on us.

"Riiiiiiiight . . . " the drunken man responded.

At this moment, we realized that this was not your typical "get spotted in public/hear snide remark" kind of situation. This guy thought we were part of the party.

"No, really," we assured our new friend. "We are crime scene investigators."

"Uhhh huuuuhhhh," was his only reply.

We showed him our badges. We showed him our police radios. Sandy showed him her expensive camera. It was all in vain. This inebriated fellow would not buy that we were who we said we were. Finally, growing weary of his verbal judo, the man rejoined the rest of his group.

Relived at his departure, we continued our chat with the gal at the front desk. She had never seen or heard anything that had frightened her, but was well acquainted with the many ghostly stories surrounding her place of employment. She recounted to us a well-known legend that tells of a woman who accidently drowned in the bathtub on her honeymoon. This tragic event occurred in room 1102. Ever since then guests have reported strange goings on in and around that room.

When our conversation with the clerk hit a lull we decided to jump on the elevator and check out the eleventh floor for ourselves before we went back to work. This course of action seemed like such a good idea at the time—that is, until the entire group of sauced partiers from the lobby decided to join us. We were literally packed in the little metal box nose to nose as we started to rise. To make matters worse, when we reached the fifth floor, the elevator suddenly jerked to a halt and would not move another inch. Neither would the doors open. The thought flashed through my head that there were too many people in this ancient elevator and that we were stuck.

This turn of events shook the revelers out of their drunken stupor and they, with one accord, began to hoot, holler, and carry on. I looked over at Sandy. She was standing toe to toe with some dude who was smiling lasciviously and telling her what a nice camera she had. She looked at me, mouthing the words, "I'm going to kill you."

After what seemed like an eternity the car commenced its upward climb and began to empty out, floor by floor. When we reached the eleventh floor we were alone. We peeked gingerly out of the elevator door. I am not sure what we expected to see—maybe "Slimer" from *Ghostbusters* coming around the corner.

We looked around for a minute, totally underwhelmed by the lack of paranormal activity, then made our way out of the building. No other calls were pending, so we made our way back to the office. It was a bit of a melancholy ride; after all, both of us had wished to experience something that would have made us part of the lore surrounding that old majestic building.

Disappointed, yet at the same time intrigued by the evening's highjinks, Sandy began some online research concerning the Ben Lomond Hotel. After reading for a while she called out to me from across the room, her voice alive with excitement. As it turned out, our evening had not been a total waste. Along with the tales of vanishing old ladies and stories of things that go bump in the night, a recurring event attributed to ghostly interference had been chronicled on several websites. You see, for reasons no one has ever been able to discern, and despite the best efforts of countless repairmen, the elevators at the Ben Lomond Hotel have a mind of their own. They run by themselves at all hours of the night and people are let off on the wrong floors, with unwanted trips to the tenth and eleventh floors frequently noted. Sometimes the elevator just simply gets stuck on random floors. Despite our initial dejection, it turns out two crime scene investigators had indeed become part of the haunted history of the Ben Lomond Hotel.

Chapter Five
Gone Fishing

If one were to believe television CSI shows, you would think that the average work day for a crime scene investigator is one rip-roaring adventure after another. Why, according to Hollywood, I should single-handedly solve a high profile homicide, take point on a SWAT raid, and then maybe jump out of a helicopter on to the back of a moving train—all before breakfast!

The reality of crime scene work is infinitely less exciting than that. Truth be told, if the producers showed the hours of paperwork to be done, the days consumed with staring at the same fingerprint, or the weeks spent meticulously reconstructing a crime scene, the show's ratings would be pretty low. No one would spend precious time watching a routine day in the life of the typical crime scene investigator.

It was exactly one of these routine days that my previously highlighted friend Mitch *thought* he was having. Mitch figured his paranormal days were in the rearview mirror. He had sold the house vexed by the troubled soul who had followed him home from a crime scene and had moved into a newly remodeled house his grandfather had owned until his passing a few years before. Mitch had also married in the meantime and was settling into domestic bliss. His enigmatic pug, "The Dude," took the move in stride and quickly settled into his new home. The only odd behavior he exhibited was a preoccupation with a room Mitch turned into his library. The dog often stood in the doorway just staring into the room.

While this behavior reminded Mitch somewhat of the dog's previous run-in with the great beyond, its frequency and severity were so much less that Mitch simply chalked it up to the eccentricities of a middle-aged pug. After all, the human residents of the house were not experiencing anything strange.

It is within this new context that we find Mitch at work one day, heading toward a call; not a politically motivated quadruple homicide, or a ten-million-dollar jewel heist pulled off by a slick band of international thieves, or the kidnapping of a celebrity's daughter, or any other thrilling adventure you might see on television. No, Mitch was headed to the kind of call that real crime scene investigators spend their days working on. Mitch was going to a business burglary, a typical call for a typical day.

The business that had the misfortune of being burglarized was a new age-type shop that sold crystals and incense, and offered psychic readings for a price. Some perpetrator had gone through a back window and removed money from a cashbox behind the front counter. Mitch had to process the scene for latent fingerprints; a pretty straightforward job.

When Mitch arrived on scene he hit the point of entry first and worked his way inside. He entered the building at the same time as a customer who was there for a "reading." Two women were working at the store at the time and the younger of the two went into a back room with the customer. The other stayed and chatted Mitch up while he processed the front counter area and cashbox. This "chatting up" is not uncommon, since most people are interested in what a crime scene investigator does and they like to watch us work and ask questions.

After a time, the other employee came out of the back room. Mitch saw she wore a troubled expression. She came up to the lady with Mitch and asked if she would come back and help her with the reading, because she was having some trouble. Her co-worker obliged, and both women left Mitch and went into the back room. Mitch, having no idea what exactly the trouble was, went on with his work, skillfully searching for clues to solve the case.

It was not long until both women returned from the back room and walked toward Mitch. This time both women looked rather embarrassed. When they reached him, the older gal opened her mouth as if to speak and then closed it again without uttering a word. After a bit she opened her mouth again but still did not say anything. She was clearly trying hard to find exactly the right words. Finally, possibly deciding that the direct approach was the best one, she asked Mitch, "Do you . . . have a dead male friend or relative who really liked fishing?"

To say that Mitch was taken aback by this question would be an understatement. Of all the strange and random questions one might get asked in a day, this question certainly ranks up there with the strangest and the most random.

The best Mitch could muster was a feeble, "Huh?"

The younger of the two employees, realizing the sheer impossibility of answering such a question on the fly, came to Mitch's rescue with an explanation.

"Well, you see," she proffered. "While I was trying to do a reading back there . . . a spirit came into the room. It was a spirit who followed you here to the store. He follows you around a lot, actually. He was not trying to bother me or anything; he was just interested in what I was doing. The trouble was . . . I couldn't concentrate because of this incessant clicking noise that was associated with him. It sounded like the reel on a fishing pole. Do you know anyone like that?"

Mitch did know someone like that. He was living in his old house. His old bedroom was now Mitch's library, the room his ghost-detecting dog was constantly staring into. The person was Mitch's grandfather, who had been an avid fisherman his entire life, and apparently still was. Mitch, who had thought his supernatural troubles were behind him, put two and two together and realized that instead of ghosts following him home from work, one had followed him to work from his house, where the spirit apparently hung out.

Not knowing what to do in such a situation, Mitch apologized for any inconvenience that he had caused. They assured him that no harm had been done, but requested him to ask the spirit to leave them alone so they could finish their work. In the meantime Mitch had finished his own work. He apologized again and left the building.

As Mitch walked back to his truck, he weighed this latest spiritual turn of events in his mind. Certainly having your beloved grandfather hanging around the house years after his death was less disconcerting than having a murder victim follow you home. And perhaps having already gone through a haunting had prepared him. He decided right there on the spot that he was not bothered by this latest ethereal interaction in the least.

Mitch climbed up in his truck and turned the key with a smile on his face. Popping the vehicle into reverse, he chuckled and said aloud, "Grandpa, I can't take you anywhere."

Chapter Six
The Restless Patient

When my then thirteen-year-old son came to me and announced he wanted to be a chemist I was very happy; not just because wanting to be a chemist is a very sensible thing, but because he did not want to follow me into law enforcement. Why does this make me so happy? Because law enforcement is, more often than not, a tough, miserable, and thankless job.

Let me give you my favorite example of this. One Christmas Day several years ago, while most of Christendom was enjoying the holiday with family, friends, and delicious food, I was lying on cold, hard ground with my head in a pool of ice water, trying to fish a used condom out from under a Tuff-Shed with a hockey stick. Such a yuletide scene is not likely to be immortalized on a Christmas card any time soon. When people who do not know me gush about how exciting and glamorous my job must be, I tell them that story. That ends the conversation pretty quickly.

It has been noted for years that law enforcement personnel have higher-than-normal rates of alcoholism, divorce, and suicide. Many of these problems stem from something one of my favorite criminal justice professors, Wayne Overson, warned our class about years ago. Wayne warned us that due to the singular nature of the experiences that cops and crime scene investigators have, it is easy to become slowly alienated from your family and friends. This alienation is brought about by feelings that these people from your old life can no longer understand you. One is then drawn into relationships with people in the business whom you feel do understand you, thus causing the destruction of previous associations.

Over the years, I have come to see that Professor Overson was spot on. It is no coincidence that many cops end up divorced and remarried to other cops or crime scene investigators or dispatchers. Another group that law enforcers seem drawn to is nurses. We do spend a lot of time in emergency rooms dealing with crime victims, and even though nurses are not out on the mean streets, they share the common experience of being confronted with blood, pain, and death on an almost daily basis. This, combined with a dark sense of humor that is almost a required survival mechanism, makes cops and nurses a natural fit. And it seems this is not all that nurses have in common with us: as it turns out, nurses have their fair share of run-ins with the supernatural as well.

It stands to reason that hospitals would be haunted; after all, people die in them all the time, and usually not in a pleasant fashion. Our local hospitals are no exception, and it is from one of our local hospitals that a very interesting story comes.

Several winters ago, a man in his thirties was brought into the emergency room. He had been found crumpled up in a heap on the side of the road. He was ice cold, and for all intents and purposes, dead. In medical jargon, he was in "full arrest." Nevertheless, the ER staff launched a heroic effort to revive and save the man. They worked the man for a good forty-five minutes, trying to get his heart started, but in the end they had to let him go. The hospital had a problem, though. They did not know who this poor, unfortunate fellow was. He had come in as a John Doe with no identification on him. All he had was a small brown backpack containing only a few personal items. Hospitals usually like to know whom they are treating. On one hand, they need to notify the patient's family, especially in cases of death. On the other, they need to know where to send the bill for their services. Here they were with that exact problem on their hands.

After the frenetic action of lifesaving had ceased, the nurses returned to their normal routine and began checking on the other patients. It is a fact of life in emergency rooms that the most critical patients get the most attention and those who are not as badly off are sometimes put on the back burner. It is called triaging, and such was the case that day.

Immediately next to the room where the life-and-death drama had played out was another room containing an elderly female with breathing problems. Accompanying this stricken woman was her adult daughter. When a nurse named Cindy went in to check on the mother, she saw that the daughter was visibly upset and shaking. She asked what the matter was. The daughter at first seemed hesitant, then blurted out, "I'm not sure if this is helpful, but the man in the next room—he was here in this room!"

"Ma'am," Cindy replied, "the man in the next room is dead. He was dead when they brought him in."

"I know," the daughter responded. "This kind of thing has happened to me before, albeit not as intense. Although I could not see him, he had a hand on each of my shoulders and was talking right in my face. He was frantic. He told me he did not want to die."

The daughter went on to tell Cindy that she had heard the action in the next room and had known something serious was going down. Not long after, the spirit of the John Doe had come in to her and was practically yelling in her face, his hands clamped down on her shoulders. He was frantic. He had not wanted to die, and he was very worried about his mother and sister being taken care of. There had been another death in the family recently and he worried this would be too much for them. He told the shocked woman that he had been drinking heavily, and that this had led him there to the hospital. He kept insisting that he did not want to die and did not want to go back into the room where his body was. He wanted her to tell his family that he was so, so sorry for the way things turned out. He begged her to relay this message.

Even though she had not seen him when he came in, or ever had seen him, she was able to describe him. Mind you, she did not know this guy from Adam; nevertheless, she was able to accurately describe a tattoo on his arm and correctly place a scar and an earring. That being said, it was the last bit of personal information she provided that piqued Cindy's interest the most.

"Oh, and he told me his name," she said. "He said his name was Thomas."

When she had finished her story, which Cindy wrote down on the hospital chart, it was time for the older woman to be moved to a different section of the hospital, so the mother and daughter left. After their departure, Cindy walked slowly back into the room where the John Doe was still laying on the high-tech hospital bed. She turned the story she had just heard over and over in her mind. Had the spirit of this man really spoken to this other woman, she wondered?

At this point, the hospital had still made no headway trying to ascertain the identity of the man. Trying to help, Cindy picked up the little backpack that had come in with him and looked inside. As was noted before, there was no official identification in the backpack. There was, at the bottom, a small store receipt. It had been overlooked on an initial search. Written in pen on the receipt was a name.

The name was Thomas.

Chapter Seven
The Dancing Specter

Fingerprints are one of the most tried-and-true forms of evidence for linking a suspect to a crime scene. That being said, Hollywood has left the public with the impression that a crime scene investigator can find a match on a fingerprint on any object imaginable. In the fertile imaginations of the members of the Writers Guild of America, there is no surface too textured, too wet, too dirty, or otherwise incompatible that cannot harbor a perfect fingerprint just waiting for a blue light to find it.

This could not be farther from the truth. In fact, finding a comparable fingerprint is far rarer than you think. I always consider it a happy little miracle, and finding the fingerprint is the easy part. Comparing the latent fingerprint to the known fingerprint impressions of a suspect can take hours, days, or even weeks.

What you are trying to do when comparing two fingerprints is determine if the individual characteristics that each fingerprint has, along with the spatial relationship those characteristics have with each other, are present in both prints in sufficient amounts. If they are, the same finger made both prints. If not, the same finger did not make the two prints.

This one-paragraph description does not do justice to the skill required to do such comparisons, nor to the complexity of the process. There are definite protocols that must be followed when doing such work. One of these protocols deals with the order in which the individual detail of a print is compared during the examination. When comparing the print from the crime scene with the known fingerprint impressions of a suspect, you should always examine the print from the crime scene first. Once you have found the individual detail and spatial relationships in that print, you are free to then look at the suspect print and look for the corresponding features.

The reason you proceed in this order is to avoid bias. If one examines the suspect fingerprint—which is usually clearer—first, one might try to mentally force the features found in that print to fit the features found in the less clear print from the scene. I suppose looking at the suspect's print first could be compared to taking a test. If you think you know the answer to a question in advance you might not read the question thoroughly, a practice that could lead to mistakes.

Yes, becoming fixated on one set of facts or perceptions at the expense of the whole picture can cause one to jump to erroneous conclusions. This is as true in life as it is in latent fingerprint examination.

My brother found this out for himself one night. Dave is a security officer and has been for many years. He has noted with amusement over the years that every new job he has been assigned to has its own resident ghost. This is according to the other officers who have worked those locations for many years. His compatriots have reported seeing everything from the restless spirit of a Native American chief in full regalia to a witch equipped with her very own flying broom. My brother was not sure if these other officers had really seen something or if this was a form of hazing. Nevertheless, such tales always made him a bit wary of the new site for the first little while. That being said, he himself had never seen anything strange—until one particular night.

After making his rounds, he took his place in front of the bank of monitors for the multiple security cameras keeping an eye on the building. Checking each screen individually, Dave scanned for any sign of trouble. Everything appeared in order until he got to the screen showing the view of one of the entry doors. Something on the monitor made my brother sit straight up in his chair and gulp. Floating in front of the door was what appeared to be a vaporous apparition. It just hovered there, still and unmoving.

Were the grizzled veterans of this job site correct after all? Was this building actually haunted? Dave was going to find out. He jumped out of his chair and hurried down to the corridor where he had seen the phantom standing. When he came around the bend he saw . . . nothing. No smoke. No steam. No glare. There was nothing in that hall that could account for what he saw on the screen.

Perplexed, Dave returned to his seat in front of the monitors. He was staring at the ghostly image on the screen, trying to unravel this conundrum when he saw something that utterly amazed him. No longer content to simply stand still, the specter began to move up and down like it was dancing. Dave noticed that it had commenced this gyration when the door opened and a person had entered the building. When the door closed and the person went on their way down the hall, the figure once again merely hung in the air.

Dave could not believe his eyes. Not only was this whatever-it-was visible on the closed-circuit television, but it had also reacted to the presence of a person in the hall. It had moved like it had been trying to get the person's attention. Something seriously strange was happening here. Perhaps his colleagues were right. This building might indeed be haunted. Or was it something else? Dave could not shake a nagging feeling telling him that he had missed an important detail.

Dave left his post to check the hall one more time. This time, after carefully scanning the corridor and seeing nothing, he looked up at the camera. Lo and behold, there it was—the answer to the mystery of the dancing ghost. A dusty cobweb hung in front of the camera's lens. When the air rushed in through the open door it moved in the breeze. When the door was closed, it was perfectly still. He verified this by experiment a few times and was satisfied with the results.

Laughing audibly at himself and the situation, Dave returned to his post. It is funny what a cobweb will look like when one is expecting a witch.

Chapter Eight
A Blizzard of Papers

Many policemen and policewomen start their careers in public safety working as security guards. Many also end their public safety careers working in security. The reasons for this are simple. On the front end, a young person wanting to pursue a vocation in law enforcement is usually interested in stopping crime, enforcing the law, and helping people. A wise job seeker also wants to acquire some experience in the public safety sector to build their resume. This makes a job as a security guard a natural fit for someone trying to get a position with a police department or someone putting themselves through the police academy.

On the back end of things, cops can retire at a fairly young age compared to the rest of the labor force. Most of them are eligible to retire after twenty years, although that has changed a bit in recent years.

The trouble is, if one retires in their forties or early fifties, you are years away from qualifying for Medicare, so most people still have to work to pay for insurance. Why not put the skills you spent twenty-plus years honing to good use? Whether it is for a Fortune 500 company or the local mall, many retired cops finish their professional lives in the security field.

An ironic side note to all of this is that even though many of them started there and even more of them are going to end up there, most current officers range from slightly to ardently scornful of security guards. Go figure.

Anyway, working as a security officer is not only a good place to gain public safety experience, but it is a good place to gain paranormal experience as well. It only stands to reason that when you have people alone at night in big, scary places odd things are bound to happen. The logic of the world of ghosts basically demands it, and a friend of mine who worked night security in a historic building in downtown Salt Lake City was no exception.

The City-County building on State Street was completed in 1894, and is a marvelously ornate building. In fact, the Utah Heritage Foundation's website calls it "Utah's finest example of Richardsonian Romanesque architecture." People come from all over to take tours and revel in the grand old building's past. The trouble is, not all of its visitors leave when it is closing time.

For instance, a friend of mine named Jeremy, before he was a cop, was the night watch commander for a security company that guarded several sites around greater Salt Lake City. One of these sites was the City-County building. Part of his duties on a nightly basis was to monitor radio traffic. If he heard that any of his subordinates had questions or needed help, he would respond.

Late one night after midnight, the guard stationed at the City-County building radioed an urgent call into dispatch. With abject panic in his voice, he reported that a man was hanging out of a second story window, throwing papers everywhere. So many papers were being tossed about, he cried, that they were covering the ground like snow. He needed backup, and he needed it now, the poor fellow urged.

The panic in this man's voice alone would have spurred his comrades into action, let alone the bizarre events he portrayed. Needless to say, it was not long before Jeremy and other security officers arrived on the scene. What greeted the new arrivals was not a blizzard of papers, but rather a badly shaken comrade pointing up at a second story window that was shut tightly.

"What on earth is going on here?" Jeremy demanded.

"He was there . . . I saw him. He was right there," the guard stammered.

"Nobody is there now, pal!" Jeremy replied.

"He was there . . . throwing papers . . . everywhere," the bewildered guard responded. "The papers were covering the grass and the sidewalk—everything."

Jeremy could clearly see that there were no papers covering the grounds. There was no evidence that this man's story was true other than his demeanor, which indicated he was in shock. Jeremy suggested to the assembled guards that they go in and check and clear the building. The frightened security officer politely declined. The rest of the men went inside and searched the building. All the doors were still locked up tight. Many of them were even chained. An examination of the second floor window identified by the bewildered guard not only showed no signs of tampering, but revealed that the window was incapable of even opening at all. There was no sign at all of anyone having been in the building, let alone hanging out of the window throwing papers to the wind.

The officers trudged back outside to their waiting comrade to make a report. Jeremy told him that the coast was clear and that he could go back inside and resume his watch. The befuddled fellow thought for a minute, then replied that he would never enter that building again as long as he lived and resigned right there on the spot!

Well, this turn of events left my friend in a tight spot. There was now no one to cover the rest of the shift and none of the other guards stepped forward and volunteered. As the watch commander, it fell on Jeremy to fill in until the day shift came on. So it was that not long after, Jeremy found himself alone inside the City-County building—a building that had just caused one of his subordinates to up and quit.

After checking all the doors again and clearing all the rooms for the second time in an hour, Jeremy relaxed. What could happen, he reasoned. He had the only set of keys into the building. None of his fellow guards could sneak up on him and mess with him. He was completely alone. Firm in this conviction, he felt the call of nature. Jeremy leisurely strolled into one of the many bathrooms inside the building. He chose a stall, entered, removed his gun belt—which he hung on the stall door—and settled in. The building was perfectly still.

Suddenly Jeremy heard a sound that certainly got his attention; he clearly heard the bathroom door open and then close. Now on edge, he waited for what was going to happen next. He did not have to wait long, as all of a sudden the lights went out and Jeremy was sitting in the dark. In the darkness he lunged forward and fumbled to find his gun and flashlight. Finding both, he poked his head out of the stall door and scanned the room, his pants around his ankles. Nothing; there was nothing there. He was quite alone, which considering his state of dress was probably a good thing.

Jeremy got himself put together, and armed with his sidearm and a newfound sense of sympathy for his former coworker, checked the doors and searched the building for a third time. As before, the doors were locked and chained. There was no sign of anyone having been there. Nothing else strange happened to Jeremy that night, but seven o'clock could not come soon enough.

That morning, when Jeremy reported the night's events to his boss—the company owner—the boss confided to Jeremy that this was not the first such occurrence at that site or the first guard who had summarily quit. One poor guy had reported to dispatch that the chandelier in the main lobby was swaying and swinging so wildly that he worried it would fall to the floor. When others had responded they saw that not only was the fixture not swinging, but that it had a solid base and was not able to sway even an inch.

The boss had even had his own brush with the unexplained. He told my friend that the City-County building was one of the first contracts he had acquired when he founded the company. In those days he had taken some of the watches himself. The layout of the floors is such that each floor has two sets of stairs, one on each end of a long corridor. The corridor is not too long, and when you come up one set of stairs you can see the other set with no difficulty.

One night while on his rounds the boss ascended one set of stairs to the second floor. Looking down toward the opposite set of stairs, he was surprised to see two small children: a boy and a girl, both around five or six years old. When the children saw him, they rushed down the stairs to the first floor. Wanting to find out why in the world two children were in the building at this hour of night, he quickly turned and descended. There was no place for the kids to go. All of the doors into the various rooms were locked and there were no other stairs for them to go down. The outside doors were locked and chained. He would be able to catch them easily, he thought to himself. He was wrong. When he got to the first floor the children had vanished.

Chapter Nine
The Note

One of the most peculiar aspects of crime scene work comes from the fact that we spend a lot of time driving around town, and that once we go into a house, we may not leave for a while. Those two facts, in and of themselves, are not peculiar, but it is the combination of the two that is. Let me explain . . . you may drive past a particular house a thousand times in the process of coming and going to calls. It may catch your attention for some reason (interesting yard ornament, cool car, etc.) or it may not. Then, one day, that house that you may or may not have noticed becomes your entire world. You spend hours, days, weeks, or even in extreme cases months inside. You know the place like the back of your hand.

As my good friend and colleague Jason said of a house wherein we had spent almost every waking hour for two months: "We know that house better than the owner." Believe him, we did.

Having spent so much time analyzing a place, we do not have too many unanswered questions when we finally leave. This is not always the case. For you see, some enigmas are out of the reach of even modern forensic science.

The call started inconspicuously. I was dispatched to what is called in the business an "unattended death" in a local trailer park. An unattended death is a call where a person passes away who has not seen a doctor in recent past. In such cases, state law may mandate an investigation even if death is by natural causes. Unattended deaths are common enough calls; I did not think much of it until I pulled up in front of the trailer. All of the first responders were standing out on the porch, even though it was a cold December day in Utah. That is never a good sign.

"Stinky?" I asked as I walked toward the group, surmising that I had a severe case of decomposition on my hands.

"Yes," the lead officer responded. "But not for the normal reasons."

"Huh?" I returned.

"Mold." He replied. "Everything inside this house is covered with mold . . . including the victim."

"Mold?"

"Yup . . . Mold."

There is a strong culture of teasing in law enforcement, so I did not know if he was being serious or not as I poked my head in the door. What greeted me was a scene that would have been the envy of the most twisted horror movie set designer in all of Hollywood. Through slits in the heavy drapes covering the windows, slivers of light illuminated piles upon piles of garbage, old newspapers, empty butter tubs, dirty dishes, and old clothing. A sweep of my flashlight revealed porcelain dolls in every corner of the front room, their dark, lidless eyes staring blankly back at me through veils of dusty cobwebs. Sections of ceiling had caved in, and the only noise to be heard was the sound of slowly dripping water. I saw that the officer was not kidding; just about everything was covered with thick, green mold.

Of all the dark and depressing places I have been, this may very well have been the worst. Even my brightest LED flashlight did little to penetrate the gloom. I found that very odd at the time. Those flashlights can light up a country road in the middle of the night, but it did not even put a dent in the palpable murk. We could not have even turned on the house lights, since none appeared to be functioning.

As I walked to where the deceased woman lay, I could tell that the carpet was saturated with an unknown liquid. The stomach-turning squishing sound that accompanied each step reminded me that in my line of work, ignorance is bliss. I found myself really hoping that I was slogging through water.

The woman's bedroom was no better off than the rest of the trailer and neither was she for that matter. She, too, was covered with mold, the same as her earthly possessions. The poor old gal had been down long enough for her face and fingertips to have begun to mummify. There had been no one to check on her. Her husband had died many years before and she had no family in the area. She had always kept to herself and her neighbors barely knew her.

I took my photographs and examined the scene. She had every appearance of someone who had died peacefully in her sleep. There were no signs of a struggle and no visible injuries. When I completed my part of the investigation, I went outside to get some fresh air and wait for the medical examiner. Often on death investigations you will hang out where the body is, looking around, counting pills, or something while you are waiting. Not this place. Coming out of this scene was like popping your head out from the water after holding your breath for a long time. You just wanted out.

On my way out of the door, I did notice on the floor of the kitchen a book about haunted places in America. It was devoid of mold and relatively dust free, leading me to believe that she had probably read that book fairly recently. I can't explain why, but seeing that book enhanced the overall creepiness of the scene.

It was not long before the medical examiner and the body transport folks showed up and did their thing, and this unfortunate woman was on her way to autopsy, which was to show no sign of foul play. As is my practice, I went back inside for my final walk-through. It is a good idea to check the scene one last time in case you missed something. And miss something I had. On her bedroom door, I noticed a piece of paper that looked out of place, hanging among yellowing pictures and old newspaper clippings. The top edges were curled in on themselves, but the paper was not discolored or stained like the other objects on the door. Illuminated by the beam of my flashlight, I could see something written on the paper.

I rolled the edges back and read five simple words posing a question that made my head reel. What on earth did this note mean? I immediately thought of the book I had seen on the floor of the kitchen. Was her interest in ghosts related to this note, or was it just a coincidence? I could not wrap my mind around it.

The content of the note even made me question our conclusions regarding this case. Had she really been *alone* in the dark when she died? In a shaky yet legible hand was written a plea to someone or something: "WHO OR WHAT ARE YOU?!?"

48

Chapter Ten
The Empty Chair

When the practice of having a specific crime scene investigation unit within a police department was in its infancy, these groups were populated almost exclusively by patrol officers. These were not just any patrol officers; it was joked that these early pioneers of our trade were the "nearly dead" or the "brain dead."

It was only partially a joke. More often than not, if a beat cop was too old to physically perform his duties or was a "screw up," he would be sent to CSI, where he could do the least amount of damage. Although some of them went on to do great work and pave the way for us today, it is safe to say that, initially, not a lot of importance was attached to education.

Fortunately for all of us, this paradigm has gradually changed. As time passes, more and more emphasis has been placed on education in general, and on quality in the forensic sciences in particular. Several events have been the catalyst for this shift.

The first game-changer was a string of Supreme Court decisions in the 1960s, dealing with due process, search and seizure, and protection from the government. One of the more crucial and influential decisions from that time is *Miranda v. Arizona 1966*. In this decision, it was determined that the defendant did not understand his right against self-incrimination and should have been advised of those rights. The resulting overturned conviction caused a radical change in how interrogations were conducted and led to the now famous "Miranda Warning" that all of us who grew up watching eighties police shows are so familiar with. William Shatner as TJ Hooker did it the best.

With it now harder to obtain confessions, forensic science was viewed as the next-best method for guaranteeing convictions, and more thought and resources were given to the concept of scientifically evaluated evidence.

With this change, you needed more scientifically trained individuals doing the evaluating, not simply the "nearly dead" or the "brain dead." Criminal justice and forensic science programs started springing up at universities all over the nation.

Another shake-up came with the OJ Simpson trial of the nineties. If *Miranda* was the affirmation of the importance of scientifically evaluated evidence, OJ was the reaffirmation. After watching those poor forensic scientists get torn apart by a slick and well-funded defense dream team, everyone in the business felt vulnerable. Forensic practitioners redoubled their efforts. I was a forensic student at the time and we all saw the future and worked harder. There had never been more of an emphasis on education and excellence.

This brings us to the place many police officers, crime scene investigators, and lab technicians were educated: the Social Science Building on the campus of Weber State University. If you are practicing one of the aforementioned law enforcement disciplines in the intermountain west, chances are you spent some time in that large, square, multi-floored building.

Completed in 1973, the Social Science building houses the Criminal Justice, Geography, History, Political Science, Philosophy, Psychology, Sociology, Anthropology, Social Work, and Gerontology departments, and according to the school's website, it is visited by four thousand students a day. It seems that these seekers of knowledge are not its only visitors.

I had heard rumors for quite a while that the Social Science building was haunted. These vague rumblings were replaced by first-hand accounts one night when I spoke with one of the building's longtime custodians named Sandy. She told me that while she had felt peculiar feelings all over the building, the epicenter of strangeness was on the second floor.

This revelation was of particular interest to me, since I had spent the bulk of my time on that very floor. You see, the Criminal Justice Department and the student crime lab were situated on the second level. In fact, the actual working Northern Utah Crime Lab had been located there. The evidence lockers are still right there in the hall, visible today.

When pressed on exactly what had taken place, Sandy recounted several odd occurrences to me. For starters, one night, a vacuum cleaner that was clearly not plugged in turned on by itself.

Another night, after all the students had gone home, she and a colleague had finished cleaning and straightening the chairs in a classroom. This particular classroom has long tables stretching across the width of the room with loose chairs underneath. As they left the room, all the chairs had been pushed completely under the tables.

When they looked back into the room not more than ten minutes later, they saw that all of the chairs on the back row of tables had been moved from beneath the table. They were not simply pulled out. The chairs were arranged in a pattern, such that all of the chairs seemed to be divided into sets of two. The front of each chair in the set was pointing toward the front of the other chair, set at a forty-five-degree angle forming chair triangles. This was the case for the whole back row of chairs.

Still another time, Sandy saw on the floor of this same classroom a pen lying between the rows of tables toward the front of the room. Wanting a clean floor, she walked toward the pen so she could pick it up. When she got to the row where she had seen the pen mere seconds before it was simply gone.

Sandy has heard her name called in dark and lonely halls and seen shadowy figures out of the corner of her eye—and Sandy is not alone. It seems that most of the cleaning staff has had something bizarre happen to them. One fellow told me of a time when one of the janitors he supervised worked the overnight shift. Around five-thirty a.m., he heard noises coming from a classroom. When he came close to investigate, he heard what sounded like a history lecture being given. He could clearly make out a professor teaching and students asking questions. Considering the time of day, this man was surprised, to say the least. Classes should not be starting for another two hours or so. Wanting to know exactly what was going on and why he had not been informed of this early morning breach of protocol, he opened the door to the classroom and popped his head in. The room was empty.

These goings-on are not the strangest thing occurring in the good old Social Science Building. The honor of that distinction would have to go to a certain piece of furniture.

In one particular room in the basement, there is a chair in which the forensic science instructors will no longer allow the students to sit. It is in the front row, right side of the room, next to the wall. You see, students are creatures of habit and tend to sit in the same seat day after day. Bearing that in mind, the first semester a certain professor taught in this room, the girl who sat in that chair got into a horrible automobile accident and had to drop out of school. The next semester the girl who sat there got cancer. The semester after that, the occupant of that seat lost her mother to an unexpected illness.

One calamity can be explained away as chance. Two calamities in a row could be called a coincidence, but three calamities in a row? Not wanting to tempt fate any further, to this day, the cursed chair on the right side of the front row next to the wall is purposely kept empty.

Chapter Eleven
The Bridge

In spite of what the television CSI shows would have you believe, it is not forensic science that solves most of the criminal cases out there. The most common form of evidence presented in courtrooms across the United States is eyewitness testimony. Eyewitness testimony, in all reality, is the cornerstone of our criminal justice system.

It is a form of evidence that is not without its problems. Stress, sleep deprivation, prejudice, bad lighting, and other human weaknesses can alter the way a situation is perceived. As a general rule, having more than one witness diminishes the chance for error.

Nevertheless, having multiple witnesses does not ensure there will not be any problems. Several studies over the years have shown that eyewitnesses may change their stories if other eyewitnesses of the same event insist it happened a different way. The different recollections of a group of individuals might coalesce into a single inaccurate account.

Be that as it may, the legal system could not function without testimony provided by eyewitnesses. It is therefore crucial for investigators to take steps to mitigate the problems associated with this type of evidence. It is important for them to try and find as many witnesses to a crime or accident as possible. It is also vital to separate these witnesses and not let them talk to each other before they can tell their story. This telling might be via a formal interview, or by simply filling out a written witness statement. This way no one can compare notes, as it were, before investigators can lock them into their stories. So as a general rule, if you have multiple witnesses who have been isolated from other witnesses, you stand the best chance of getting a true version of events.

Which brings us, in a roundabout way, to two women, a mother and daughter, driving down a local thoroughfare named Riverdale Road one dark and rainy night. When they got close to the middle of one of the bridges where Riverdale Road crosses an interstate, the two women saw something startling. Standing ahead of them on the side of the road was a twenty-something-year-old woman. She had one leg on the black top and one leg over the concrete barrier that protects cars from the thirty-foot drop to the highway below. As the car approached the girl, the occupants of the vehicle saw that the girl had dark hair and was dressed only in shorts and a T-shirt, which did not seem like appropriate attire for such an inclement night. The precariously perched youngster seemed to be crying and was covering her eyes with one hand. They both wondered what on earth this poor thing was doing on the side of the road.

Deciding quickly that something did not look right, the driver of the vehicle pulled the car to the side of the road a little past the damsel in distress. When the two women in the car got out and looked back, their fears were confirmed: the young woman was gone. Both assuming she had jumped, our good Samaritans ran to the edge of the bridge and looked over, expecting to see a battered and broken body on the road below. To their mutual surprise there was no one there. The women could not understand. The only way off the bridge where the girl had gone over the edge was a precipitous drop. There was no ledge or embankment she could have gotten on to after she went over the barrier, just a straight drop. What had happened to this despondent girl?

Totally freaked out at this point, they did the only thing they could think of: they called the police. Two Riverdale police officers responded to the scene of the apparent suicide. The strange incident was explained to the officers and a detailed description of the girl was offered. The officers went to the edge of the bridge and shined their powerful police flashlights on to the pavement below. Up and down they panned their lights. Nothing but passing cars was seen on the blacktop below.

After completing a thorough search, one of the officers sighed and said to the other, "I told you it was a ghost."

Stunned by this remark, the two frightened women asked what the officer meant. She reluctantly explained to them that this was the fifth time in two months that officers had been called to that exact spot. Each time, witnesses saw a young woman matching the description given by the mother and daughter, crying on the side of the road with one leg over the barrier. Even the clothing was the same. Each of the five times motorists had pulled over to offer help, and seeing that she was not there, concluded that the girl had jumped. Each time the police were called. Each time a search yielded nothing. The officer concluded they must be dealing with a ghost.

According to the rules of handling eyewitnesses, this case is a solid one, with five independent accounts verifying the same story. But what is really going on here? Is this some tormented spirit repeatedly acting out the last desperate act of her life? When I later talked to one of the responding officers—a veteran of many years—no suicide remotely matching those details could be remembered. It seemed no one on the force could recall an event of which passersby were now seeing the shadow. That does not mean that one dark and stormy night you will not see something you do not expect on the side of Riverdale Road.

Chapter Twelve
The Dog and the Sock

One of the biggest misconceptions fostered by television crime shows surrounds the concept of the foot chase. On television, when a police officer chases a bad guy on foot, said chase goes on forever and ever. The chase also involves a breathtaking series of death-defying feats. The hunted and the hunter run across half of the city. They climb to the top of tall buildings and jump to other tall buildings. They leap off bridges on to moving trains. They have gun battles while running through a crowded square. You get the point: you have seen the shows. As fantastical as all those actions may seem, the most unrealistic aspect of the television foot pursuit is the fact that the officer's uniform shirt does not come untucked even the slightest bit during the whole process. I can't even bend over and pick a shell casing up off the ground without my shirt coming untucked, but that is a different matter altogether.

Anyway, the reality of foot pursuits bears little resemblance to those presented by Hollywood. In the real world, a chase is a relatively brief affair. If the perpetrator is not caught within the first thirty seconds of the chase, he probably won't be. There are many reasons for this, but one of the main ones can be summed up as follows: *you* try to sprint and catch someone who does not want to be caught while he is wearing shorts and basketball shoes and you are wearing a heavy vest that restricts your lung function and twenty pounds of gear strapped around your waist.

Officers do catch their fair share of suspects, though, especially when the quarry is carrying a greater burden than the heavily laden officer. Two officers told me once about a time they had tried to waylay a rather rotund fellow. When they ordered this man to halt, he fled from them. The two officers watched in amusement as the ne'er-do-well huffed and puffed away from them at a snail's pace. Not knowing whether to simply laugh or "run" after the man, they did not have to weigh their options for long: after no more than one hundred feet, the fleeing subject dropped to his knees and gave up. He was barely able to gasp out his surrender through lips that had turned a sickly shade of blue.

This example is the exception rather than the rule. To reiterate, most foot pursuits end with the officer coming up empty-handed if he does not grab the person early on in the chase, and as far as I can tell, this state of affairs is fairly universal.

A story was related to me recently that leads me to wonder if the brave officers patrolling the mean streets of south central Los Angeles do not face hindrances during foot pursuits beyond those of the average police officer. You see, many of the foot chases in that part of the city end with the fugitive turning into a dog.

That last statement certainly demands explanation, and you shall have it. For the 300 or so officers of the Southeast Division of the LAPD—affectionately known as the 108th Street Division—a foot chase begins like it does everywhere. Someone who may or may not be up to no good sees police personnel and runs away from them, despite being told to halt. Like cops all over the country, the 108th Street Division officers take off after the suspect if they want him badly enough. It is pretty much standard procedure everywhere to try to radio in to dispatch and announce that one is engaged in a foot pursuit while running, give your location, and describe the general direction of the chase. After these formalities have been tended to, any good officer will try his or her best to catch the bad guy.

At this point things often take a bizarre twist on the gloomy and dangerous streets of south central Los Angeles. It just so happens that four, five, and sometimes even six times a night an officer is right on the heels of a fleeing subject—I mean, right on their heels; we are talking only twenty feet behind a runner—when the subject ducks into an alley or behind the corner of a building. As the officer rounds the same corner only seconds later, he finds the fugitive vanished into thin air. There is no sight of him, not the sound of feet smacking the pavement somewhere in the dark or the distant rattling of a chain link fence.

It is not necessarily what the officers do not see that makes this story so bizarre, but what they do see. Without fail, when a runner simply seems to evaporate, a dog is found in his place. Certainly it is not uncommon in economically depressed areas of larger US cities to find numerous stray dogs roaming the streets. This point cannot be argued. These mystery dogs do not act like your run-of-the-mill castoff slum dog.

For one, the animals never seem startled when an officer rounds a corner in the middle of the night and almost tramples them. The dogs won't flinch, yelp, or growl; they merely look calmly up at the officers. The officer who described this phenomenon to me said that many times the dogs look as though the whole situation rather amuses them.

Second, the dogs often bear an uncanny resemblance to the person the officer had been chasing. If the suspect was more clean-cut looking the dog appears well-groomed. On the other hand, if the suspect looks like he has not bathed since Bill Clinton carried his own golf clubs, the dog is dirty and mangy.

Finally, there is the fact that many times the animals had objects usually associated with humans in their immediate vicinity. Sometimes a shoe was on the ground next to the dog. Other times a shirt, or socks, or a cell phone was at their feet. These odds and ends were not soiled, wet, nor damaged, as if they had been a canine's chew toy; they were simply arrayed around the animal.

As stated, this has happened all the time, multiple times every shift, every night of the year. It was so commonplace that it did not perturb the officers in the slightest. When such a transformation occurred almost before their very eyes, the cops indifferently radioed in to dispatch and reported that the person they were chasing had turned into a dog. The other officers of the division did not snicker when they heard such radio traffic. Why should they? After all, they had the same thing happen to them many times before. It was not seen as an excuse or a joke. The officers did not even really try to understand what it all meant. It was just seen as a fact of doing business in that rough part of town.

So what really is going on down the back alleys of Los Angeles? Are we actually to believe that there are shapeshifters or skin-walkers lurking among the ranks of Los Angeles gangs? Or rather, is this all some common mythology concocted by officers who routinely let suspects slip through their fingers? One possible telling point is that although the officer who recounted these events to me worked in another division of the LAPD, the suspects only turn into dogs in south central Los Angeles. Suspects get away from cops all the time. Why is it only in the 108th Street Division that this marvel occurs?

There is one group that knows what is going on, and they are not talking. They simply wag their tails.

Chapter Thirteen
Scratches

My very seasoned and pragmatic lieutenant, Doug Coleman, has a saying, "If it ain't written down, it didn't happen." What Doug is talking about here is proof. You gotta have it.

While that little gem of wisdom applies to many aspects of life, it is of particular importance in law enforcement. In the criminal justice system in the United States, one can't simply pronounce that someone committed a crime and then lock them up for years; we have to be able to prove it.

Testimonial evidence is the most common type of evidence presented in courts today. It is not, however, the most sought-after kind of evidence. Considering the problems inherent in eyewitness testimony, prosecutors feel much more confident going into a trial when they have some physical evidence tucked into their belt. Good physical evidence can turn an iffy case into a surefire win for the prosecution, provided the meaning and context of that evidence is adequately explained to the jury.

Physical evidence can literally be anything. It can range from something as small as one skin cell to something as big as an aircraft carrier, or anything in between. Physical evidence may also be something you cannot actually hold in your hand. A photograph of a transitory item of evidence, such as a shoe print in snow or a bite mark on skin, is as valid a form of evidence as an actual object, as long as proper forensic photography procedures were followed while making said photograph and an appropriate legal foundation is laid when it is admitted into court.

What would happen if one were to accidently delete the photos of an important piece of short-lived evidence, such as the aforementioned shoe print in snow? Could one still go into court and adequately prove that a suspect's boot made the footwear impression in question? Of course not. That evidence, no matter how good, is gone, and therefore useless. This hypothetical situation takes us back to Lt. Coleman's maxim: because we no longer have documentation of the shoe print in the snow, it might as well have never existed.

While this paradigm certainly holds true for a mundane residential burglary case where we try to prove that so-and-so broke into a house one snowy evening, it is doubly true for one of the most hotly contested issues of the day: do ghosts really exist? Wouldn't it be nice to have some definitive photographic or video evidence proving once and for all that there is life beyond the grave and that spirits roam the earth? Well, thanks to a nearby paranormal hotspot we have such evidence . . . almost.

On the outskirts of Layton, Utah, sits a place known to the locals as Hobbs Hollow. Hobbs Hollow is a lovely wooded area just off a main highway. Inside the hollow sits a large pond built in the early 1900s for irrigation purposes. Hobbs Pond is a magnet for locals who want to swim, fish, and hang out.

As bucolic and pleasant as Hobbs Pond may sound, tragedy is also associated with it. The pond has some serious undercurrent issues, and is therefore a dangerous place to swim. There are many instances of people drowning in Hobbs Pond, including a well-documented case of an eleven-year-old boy back in 2004. It is no wonder that Hobbs Hollow now sports vehicle-restricting gates and a myriad of "NO TRESSPASSING" and "NO SWIMMING" signs.

Considering all of the bad things that have happened there, it is no surprise that many eerie stories surround Hobbs Hollow, nor that it is a hotspot for ghost hunters. Some of them go for the thrill of it. Others want to land on the Discovery Channel, or find fodder for their blogs. Whatever the reason, they go there in droves with cameras and video recorders, trying to capture some bit of proof that ghosts are real. One might warn these paranormal investigators to be careful what they wish for.

Not too long ago, a group of young men in their late teens snuck into the hollow one night. Armed with their cell phone cameras for documentation purposes, they went to find out if Hobbs Pond deserved its haunted status.

Many of the urban legends concerning the various drowning cases assert that some of the bodies were never recovered from the murky depths. As unlikely as this would be for a shallow, man-made pond, this scenario perhaps stirred the imagination of the boys as they scanned the gloom.

It was a cool night, and a layer of mist had formed just above the surface of the dark waters. This is nothing out of the ordinary, and the boys paid little attention to the meteorological feature. They simply watched and waited with their cameras at the ready, not quite knowing what they were waiting for.

Standing quietly in the dark at a place that carried a reputation for terror like Hobbs Pond, one might expect flights of fancy to occur. A breath of wind could be mistaken for a spectral voice, the call of a night bird could be heard as a ghostly cry for help, or a raccoon going about his nightly rounds in the undergrowth could mimic the approach of a vengeful demon. There are many things that go bump in the night that can be explained away. What happened to our would-be ghost hunters is probably not one of them.

As the young men stood there, one of them noticed that the mist above the water was not acting like normal mist should act. Slowly, almost imperceptibly, it had begun to coalesce toward the center of the pond. When this phenomenon was brought to the attention of the other members of the group, they all watched as the mist not only began to accumulate, but to mound up, slowly creating a growing hill of fog. Then, to the amazement and horror of all, the hill of mist began to morph into human form. Steadily it took the shape of a woman with a long dress and began to move ominously toward the group gathered on the shore.

The boys decided they had had enough ghost hunting for the evening. They broke ranks and ran toward their car parked up the hill by the highway. One of the fellows, not wanting to completely abandon his ghost hunting plans, held his cell phone over his shoulder and snapped a picture back towards the pond as he fled the scene.

When they were well away from Hobbs Hollow and had a chance to catch their breath, the one who took the picture pulled his phone out. He wanted to see if his last-ditch effort had captured an image of the spooky fog. To his utter amazement, he had photographed something even more frightening. Clearly visible on the screen of his cell phone was a ghostly face, and it did not look happy at all. To make matters worse, that face was not off in the distance somewhere, but right behind the boy, close enough to have reached out and grasped him in its spectral arms if it had wanted to.

Mission accomplished, they had their evidence proving the existence of ghosts, right? These amateur ghost hunters could plaster this image all over social media and become famous, right? Well, maybe—if they had kept the picture. You see, the events of the night had so unsettled our photographer, especially the fact that an apparition had been so hot on his heels, that after showing it around a bit he deleted the image. It upset him too badly to have it there on his phone; the only way he could feel better was to get rid of it altogether. The proof they had sought vanished into the night, just like the strange cloud of mist.

This group of spiritual sleuths should consider themselves lucky compared to another group who set their sights on Hobbs Hollow, for while the first group were chased unceremoniously away from the pond, at least they did not have anything follow them home.

The expedition started out routinely enough: a group of friends, including a young Weber State forensic science student who eventually became a colleague of mine, grabbed a video camera one night and headed toward Hobbs Pond. They spent some time at the water's edge, filming the location and watching for anything spooky. For a while nothing appeared to be going on. There were no ghostly sights seen or sounds heard, and eventually they gave up and headed home.

Back at the apartment of the owner of the video camera, the assembly decided to plug the camera into the television and watch their video recording, even though they felt it had been a fruitless endeavor. While the video played, the friends chatted and laughed, barely paying attention to the dark, blurry footage.

As the recording neared its end the owner of the apartment called for quiet. He thought he had heard something on the video. You could have heard a pin drop in the room as he rewound the recording and cranked the volume on the television up as loud as it would go. Then, clear as a bell, everyone in the room heard the voice of a young boy issuing from the speakers of the television. The boy whispered only one word, "Hello?" Nalleli, my co-worker, heard it with her own ears. She describes the voice as that of a child who, playing hide-and-go-seek, suddenly feels very alone and calls out to see if anyone is near. To this day it gives her goosebumps just to recount the story.

When the group of friends heard the voice it sent chills running down their backs. "Did you hear that?" they all asked each other at once. No one had heard or seen anything at the pond to make them believe there had been a child hiding in the bushes nearby. In stunned silence they played the recording over and over, trying to convince themselves that the white noise of the amplified recording was playing tricks on their ears. Every time there was the unmistakable "Hello?"

When all of the rational explanations for the voice on the tape had been examined and then discarded the screaming started. After the screaming there was some swearing. The would-be ghost hunters had inadvertently proven the veracity of the old saying, "Be careful what you wish for—you may get it!"

Eventually, after the tumult had ceased, the young adventurers set the video aside and called it a night. Surely they could all put the evening's fright behind them and go back to their normal lives—everyone except the owner of the apartment, that is. Strange things began to happen in his residence. At times areas of his apartment felt ice cold, no matter how long he left the heater on. He began to have trouble sleeping, and was overcome with feelings of dread and fear for no particular reason. Then he began to notice random scratches inexplicably appearing on his back. He saw them when he got out of the shower and could not imagine for the life of him where they came from. Nothing from his work or personal life could account for the thin red marks that started by his right shoulder and terminated midway down his back on his left side. They did not necessarily hurt, but their appearance horrified him.

With an increasing sense of alarm in his life, this poor fellow woke up unexpectedly one night and his eyes immediately went to a stack of papers on the dresser by his bed. Without warning the entire stack was thrown across the room. There were no windows open, nor was any fan blowing in the room. There was simply no reasonable explanation for the explosion of papers.

This was the last straw. Having increasingly had the feeling that the strange goings-on in his apartment were somehow related to the chilling voice on the videotape, he erased the entire recording. He hoped that this act would end his nightmare. As it turned out, it did.

After the recording was destroyed his life returned to normal. No more mysterious scratches appeared on his back. No more stacks of papers were thrown around the place. Everything was as it had been, except for the fact that he never went ghost hunting again.

So once again, there existed compelling evidence from Hobbs Hollow that spirits are among us, and once again, with the push of the delete button, it was gone. Wouldn't this voice from beyond the grave have silenced skeptics once and for all? Maybe so, but in the words of my lieutenant: "If it ain't written down, it didn't happen."

Chapter Fourteen
The Missionaries

Many of my colleagues keep a running total of how many rookie cops they have "christened." When I say christened, I mean make the new officer somehow get up close and personal with the subject of their first death investigation. For example, there are people whose job it is to bag and move deceased individuals for the purpose of getting them to autopsy. Let me just say when there is a rookie on scene, the transport guys are not bagging and picking much up. The new officer gets that experience.

It is a funny thing; a kid right out of the academy is brimming with confidence and courage. They are ready to draw their weapon to defend themselves or others, or race around town in a squad car, pursuing a dangerous felon. Most of them are not ready to see, smell, and touch a severely decomposed corpse. Several rookies have not survived their first encounter with a grizzly death scene, and have turned in their gun and badge a day or two later. Courage, it seems, has many faces, and each of us possesses more of one form and less of another. What terrifies or mortifies one person barely registers with the person next to them.

And so it is with a particular veteran police officer, Tyler, from a local agency. This guy is tough—I mean, I once saw him lay out a pugilistic 260-pound wife beater with a single punch. He is the type of cop you do not want to mess with, and fear is not usually in his professional vocabulary. Nevertheless, one night he ran smack into a situation that put it there.

It was just a routine night shift for Tyler; in fact, it was almost over. To stay alert and awake for the last few hours he was running radar, trying to catch some speeders. Suddenly, the still of the early morning was shattered by the blood-curdling scream of a woman. Now fully awake and alert, Tyler listened intently to see if he could hear it again and determine its origin. It came again, and he followed the noise into a nearby backyard. As he got closer, it sounded like the woman was arguing with someone. Domestic arguments and abuse are some of the more common types of calls to which an officer responds, and so Tyler assumed this was the case at hand and got into a certain frame of mind.

When Tyler came around the corner of the house, he only saw a single person. It was a female seated on a chair inside of a sun porch attached to the back of the house. It was then that some dread crept into his normally stalwart heart. You see, the whole scene just seemed to have been plucked right out of a Hollywood horror movie. The woman was slumped over in the chair, and her long, dark hair was pulled over her face. There was a pillar of mucus emanating from her nose and stretching over a foot in length toward the floor. She swayed back and forth and urgently argued with an unseen antagonist. A nearby radio blared "death metal" so loud that he could not really make out what she was saying.

As he watched her, Tyler started to feel worse and worse about the whole situation. It was certainly not that he feared for his physical safety; rather, he felt he was observing something—for lack of a better word—evil. Be that as it may, Tyler had a job to do, so he approached the woman. After announcing his presence and identity, he asked the woman if she needed any assistance. She did not look up. He asked again even louder, ensuring that his voice was heard above the loud music. This time she blurted out, while still not looking up at him, that she was being tortured by the devil and that she was trying to save the officer's life. With this disclosure, Tyler felt the hair on the back of his neck stand straight up. His feelings matched her words, and that disconcerted this brave officer more than I am sure he would care to admit.

After trying to discuss the nature of the woman's problems and getting nowhere in the process except more freaked out, Tyler finally asked a very un-cop-like question. The inquiry was made out of sheer desperation. He asked this woman, who had not as of yet looked up at him, if she wanted him to call the missionaries for her, which in predominantly Mormon Utah is roughly equivalent to calling a priest. At this suggestion the woman's head shot up so fast it startled Tyler. Not only did this suggestion get her attention, it apparently pleased her greatly. She smiled grimly under the snot icicle hanging from her nose and said, "Yeeeesssss."

That response was just about all Tyler could take. For reasons he cannot entirely explain, a tangible sense of fear gripped him. He left the woman to her mutterings and attempted to see if anyone else was home. Scared as he was, he had a duty to perform, and needed to get to the bottom of what exactly was happening in that sun porch during that last darkest hour before dawn.

Maybe his reaction was due to the overall cinematic creepiness of the situation. When you feel like you have walked out of reality and into a Hollywood horror movie, it can be disconcerting. I know—it has happened to me. It may be argued that Tyler, having been reared in a religious culture and raised on stories of holy men casting demons out of people, misconstrued a simple case of mental illness. Then again, perhaps he literally did feel the manifestation of a force that cannot be combated with flesh or steel. After all, discretion is the better part of valor, and not even the toughest cop in the world can knock out the devil with just one punch.

Chapter Fifteen
The Black Veil

One of the charms of working as a crime scene investigator is having literally no idea what might befall you on a given shift. An investigator could spend a typical day fingerprinting cars or find themselves flying in a military helicopter heading deep into the mountains to process a clandestine marijuana-growing operation. A crime scene investigator could spend their day sitting in the office doing paperwork, or out on a harbor patrol boat recovering a murder victim from the ocean. You could find yourself plying your trade within the cardboard walls of the most abject hovel or surrounded by marble in a palatial mansion. Your camera viewfinder has held the image of movie stars and the homeless alike. One just never knows.

So it was one day when my comrade of many years, Jason, and I found ourselves, fingerprint brushes in hand, inside an ornate mausoleum. I had never been to a crime scene in a mausoleum before, and as of this writing have not been to one since. Why were we there, you ask? Someone had removed a glass plate covering one of the niches containing the urns and made off with a gold wristwatch that had been interred with the earthly remains of the timepiece's owner. Talk about your bad karma!

We had been dispatched to the mausoleum to see if we could find any fingerprints on the glass panel in an attempt to ascertain the identity of the grave robber. At first, Jason and I were very intent on the task at hand and paid little attention to our surroundings. As the sun began to set, causing long shadows to be cast across the polished stone floor of the otherwise empty building, our mood began to perceptibly change. I can't remember which one of us asked this, but the question was raised, "Do you remember that movie *Phantasm*?"

"Yup," the other one of us gulped.

Neither of us really remembered what the movie was actually about; I was eight and Jason was seven when it was released. We only remembered that it had a knife-laden metallic sphere that flew around a mausoleum and killed people. I suppose standing there in a very similar place at dusk is all we needed to remember.

We were about done at that point, so we stowed our equipment and exited the building without lingering. Things such as the generation of field notes and the labeling of fingerprint cards could wait . . . wait until we were safely out of range of any flying death spheres. And although we personally did not see any such strange objects, it appears that the funeral home and cemetery containing this mausoleum is no stranger to the unexplained.

Years ago, I was surprised to learn that many mortuaries have people living at them full time. Usually college students lured by cheap or free rent, these folks keep an eye on the grounds and go out in the middle of the night, when the full time funeral directors are asleep, to pick up new "customers." The apartments they live in are near or actually in the mortuaries themselves. Such was the case with a friend of mine named Jeremy; a different Jeremy than the security guard from the City-County building.

When a young, newly-married college student, Jeremy lived and worked at the very funeral home where the aforementioned mausoleum stands. His living quarters were right above the part of the building where the deceased are prepared for burial. He and his wife had their first child three months prior, and he had settled into a happy routine of work, school, and fatherhood.

One day, he was downstairs in the mortuary when he heard a baby cry. Children of different ages have distinctive cries, and Jeremy thought that the cry sounded like the cry of his three-month-old daughter. It was not your run-of-the-mill cry: the child sounded frantic. It was the kind of cry that makes the hair on the back of a parent's neck stand up.

Being the conscientious new father that he was, he ran upstairs to see what was the matter with his daughter and see if his wife needed any help. Arriving at his apartment, he poked his head in the door and asked his wife if their child was okay. His wife looked surprised and responded that nothing was wrong with the child and that she was sleeping soundly in the other room.

Confused but satisfied, Jeremy went back downstairs into the mortuary and went about his business. A few minutes later, he heard the hysterical cry of a three-month-old baby again, clear as day. He ran upstairs again. Perhaps his wife had been distracted and not heard their daughter the first time. Something sounded terribly wrong with the child and he had to find out what it was. Once again, his wife assured him that the baby was sleeping peacefully and that she had not heard as much as a peep out of her.

Jeremy marched downstairs and went back to work. He must be hearing things, he assured himself. But then, not long after, he heard the cry a third time. As with the previous two times, the child sounded apoplectic. This time, though, a peculiar fact finally registered in Jeremy's mind. It was something that he had noticed the previous two incidents but had not registered. Although he could hear the child's cry distinctly, it possessed an ethereal, far off quality, like a voice carried across a lake by the wind.

Had Jeremy's daughter been the second, or especially third child, he probably would have left well enough alone at this point, but being a first-time dad, he dutifully ran up the stairs to his apartment a third time to check on his baby. As with the previous two times, his wife assured him, with discernible annoyance, that their daughter was sleeping as peacefully as only a baby free of the guilt and regrets we adults harbor can.

This time the weirdness of it all began to weigh heavily on Jeremy's mind. He was absolutely positive that he had heard a child approximately as old as his own crying frantically. There must be another child in the building, he reasoned to himself. Determined to get to the bottom of this mystery, he sought out one of his co-workers who also lived at the mortuary. Although this fellow had no children, Jeremy thought that perhaps he was babysitting a relative.

When Jeremy found his associate, the man informed him that he was not tending any children, nor had he been. He went on to assure Jeremy that the only other child in the building, besides Jeremy's daughter, was a three-month-old baby he had picked up that morning. This unfortunate child was in the cooler at that very moment, waiting to be embalmed.

This was not the only odd thing that happened to Jeremy during his time living and working at the mortuary. Part of his daily responsibilities included checking the cemetery grounds at dusk to ensure that everyone had cleared out before dark. Jeremy had a golf cart at his disposal to facilitate this task. One evening he was about his duty with his sister along for the ride. When the two siblings came around a bend, they saw in the distance a solitary woman standing by a grave, her head bowed in profound grief. This, of course, was not an unusual sight per se, but as they got closer, the woman herself struck them as odd. She was elderly and dressed in black mourning clothing, right down to a wide-brimmed hat fully equipped with a black veil. The clothing looked old-fashioned, like something out of a British period drama on PBS. Also odd was the fact that there were no cars left parked on the grounds. They had not expected to find anyone left in the cemetery. As they got closer still, the woman did not look up or make any acknowledgment of their approach.

Although it was his job to hurry people along out of the cemetery as darkness approached, this obviously had to be done with a certain amount of tact. You can't just go up to someone in deep grief and shoo them out of the cemetery like you would teenagers out of an arcade shutting its doors for the night. The employees of the mortuary tried to let people have as much time as possible with their departed loved ones before gently reminding them it was time to leave.

As the golf cart quietly glided past the old woman, putting her at their backs, this was Jeremy's plan: give her a few more minutes and then see if she needed any help. Jeremy noted as he drove past that the grieving woman was very thin and pale. She certainly might need helping getting where she needed to go.

"In fact," Jeremy thought, "I'm going to speed this process up and see if she needs help right now."

Golf carts have quite an excellent turning radius, and it was no problem at all for Jeremy to make a quick U-turn in the middle of the narrow lane and point the cart back toward the grave where the woman had been standing only seconds before.

When he did so, the woman with the black veil was simply gone.

Chapter Sixteen
The Decoration

Every autumn my mind tends to drift to a case I was involved in a few years back. As I recall, I certainly have to say it was one of the strangest nights of my career. It also changed the way I look at Halloween decorations forever.

We were called to the scene of a very suspicious death about two weeks before Halloween. Members of the deceased family had discovered the victim in his home. He was a bloody mess, and the room where he was found looked like a tornado had hit it. It did not take us long to see that he had been most likely beaten to death and that the fight, as one-sided as it was, had occurred in the room where he had been found and nowhere else. There were no signs of forced entry into the residence.

Although random killings do take place, homicide is a very personal affair. You are statistically far likelier to be killed by someone you know *well* than by a complete stranger. I guess it can be put this way: the vast majority of the time, if someone is mad enough at you to want to kill you, they have to know you first. That being said, any good detective faced with a situation like we had with this poor unfortunate fellow would quickly try to develop a "Friends and Family" list for the victim to establish whom the victim spent time with and whether there was any bad blood between the deceased and those on the list.

In talking to the family, it did not take the detectives long to establish that the departed in this case only ever hung out with one particular guy. It seemed these two men were virtually inseparable. The family provided investigators with the name of this friend, his address, and even a description of his truck. This information fit what we were finding at the crime scene. Although our victim lived alone, there were multiple double sets of dinnerware bearing the remains of the same meals in the kitchen and two overturned chairs in front of the television near the body. It seemed apparent that this guy had a frequent single guest.

As we crime scene investigators did our thing at the crime scene a set of detectives went to find this friend. When they arrived at the address provided by the family, they noted that his truck was parked in the driveway and that there were no lights on in the house. This was not an unreasonable state of affairs, since it was around one o'clock in the morning at this point. The detectives parked, went up to the front door, and rang the doorbell. Some movement was heard inside the residence. They waited a bit, but no one came to the door. At this point they just wanted to talk to this guy. He was not necessarily a suspect; he was just at the top of the "Friends and Family" list. They had no real reason to get a warrant and kick the door down, so they looked around the outside of the house to see if anything appeared out of order. Seeing nothing amiss, they left, resolving to come back later.

Homicide investigations can be very fluid and chaotic, and this one was no different. As detectives went around town contacting other people on the list, someone decided this friend at the top of the list should be contacted again. The original set of detectives being busy, a different set of investigators made the trip to the abode of the victim's best friend. As the detectives walked up to the front of the house, something caught one of the investigator's eye. The first thought that flashed through his mind when he saw what he thought he saw was, "Man, that Halloween decoration hanging there in the carport actually looks like a dead guy. That thing is going to really freak the neighborhood kids out."

Then he took a second look. Not only did the object hanging in the carport look like a dead guy, it really *was* a dead guy. In fact, it was the guy they were looking for. There was clear evidence that he had hung himself to death. I still remember the call we got back at the original crime scene.

"Hey . . . we need some CSIs over here. We got another dead body. And you are going to love this—we think it is related!"

It did indeed turn out to be related. A search of the hanged man's house turned up bloody clothing in the washing machine. The blood belonged to the man still lying on the floor in front of his television. Our best guess at what happened is that after he had murdered his friend, our killer came home to clean up. When the first set of detectives came to his house he was there and saw them, but did not open the door. Knowing now that the cops were on to him, and that it was only a matter of time before they caught up to him, he took his own life out of a sense of guilt or fear, or maybe both. The misidentified Halloween decoration had acted as his own judge, jury, and executioner.

This case still perplexes me all these years later. Why did the friends turn on each other? What really drove one to take his own life: why not just make a run for it? These questions will forever remain unanswered, since the men who knew what actually happened took that knowledge to the grave. I do know one thing for sure; to this day, I cannot look at a large-scale, lifelike Halloween decoration without thinking of the man hanging in his carport.

Chapter Seventeen
Sweet Surrender

The CSI shows on television are mostly science fiction, and most of the time have no more realism in them than an episode of *Star Trek*. This fact has the propensity to grossly inflate the public's expectations of what is possible for the average crime scene investigator, which tends to make an already difficult job ever harder.

That being said, there have been occasions when I have actually defended aspects of these shows. The main aspect of TV crime shows that I have had to defend deals with lights, or rather, the lack of them. Several people have come to me and commented that they find it silly that the actors on various shows never turn the lights on in a room they are searching, but simply poke around with their flashlights.

I find myself assuring people that such a scenario is actually fairly realistic, although the directors do it for atmosphere and not accuracy. In real life, the reason we sometimes grope around dark rooms with flashlights dates to when we were all rookies. You see, it has been ingrained in every crime scene investigator worth their salt from the beginning of their career to leave a crime scene exactly the way it was found, at least in the first stages of processing.

If the lights in a scene are off, you leave them off. The television is on, you leave it on. If the window is open, you leave it open, and so on, until the scene has been thoroughly photographed, videotaped, and sketched. Then, and only then, are any alterations made to the crime scene.

Such a practice, while good for the integrity of the scene, can have a variety of consequences for the people working a scene. Sometimes you have a crime scene like the time we investigated a shooting inside a Walmart. It was warm, well-lit, and neutral-smelling. We also had relatively clean bathrooms close at hand, and the employees brought us donuts periodically through the night.

Such utopian crime scenes (if I am allowed even to create such a phrase) are unfortunately the exception rather than the rule. The vast majority of the time, being unwilling to alter the scene causes some type of physical discomfort ranging from mild to extreme. An example of mild discomfort would be bumping around an unfamiliar place in the dark with only your flashlight for illumination. On the extreme end, you have being cooped up with a corpse in an advanced state of decomposition and not being able to open the window and air the place out.

And then there is the emotional discomfort that keeping a crime scene in its pristine state can sometimes generate. There are times when something tremendously annoying is occurring while you are trying to concentrate. You could have a barking dog, a television playing nothing but infomercials, maybe a stuck doorbell, an obnoxious wind chime, or a blaring radio. Any one of these, or countless other annoyances, can make it very difficult to work in the short term, and even add to one's emotional scars in the long term.

Such was the case during a homicide investigation near the beginning of my career. In this tragic incident, a young woman had been murdered by her soon-to-be-ex-husband. It was a rather bloody affair, he having stabbed her more than fifty times. The victim had been trapped against her bathroom door and had perished, I feel, trying to get into that room.

As we first entered the scene, the CD player in the bedroom was playing the same song over and over again. That in and of itself is not too strange; after all, most CD players have a "repeat" function. What was a little unnerving was the song playing: "Sweet Surrender" by Sarah McLachlan. When you stand in a gruesome crime scene, hearing lyrics like, "The life I've left behind me is a cold room" and "Sweet surrender is all that I have to give" over and over again over the course of several hours, it begins to wear on you and even creep you out. It was eventually decided amongst the group that the crime scene undergo an alteration and the offending song be turned off. This was accomplished, and we went about our business.

As the days and weeks of processing went on, it became apparent that this was no ordinary crime scene. I do not know if it was the memory of that melancholy and fitting song combined with the brutal crime or something else, but we all began to feel something every time we went back into that apartment. The "something" we felt was undoubtedly our victim in this case. In thinking back on that time, I can say that the sensation was not oppressive or frightening. She was just there watching what we were doing and perhaps even cheering us on. The feeling was so real and palpable that we would all offer verbal salutations to her as we walked through the door.

"Hello," we would say, calling her by name. "We're back. We should only be a few hours today."

Now you, the reader, may find such behavior for university-trained crime scene investigators odd, and perhaps it is. All I can say to that is that a feeling is a feeling, and there are plenty of things in this big blue world of ours that we do not understand.

After about a month of work and hanging out with our new friend, we finished processing the scene. We took a myriad of evidence out of that apartment—*including* the kitchen sink—but that is a story for another type of book.

Life moved on as life does. The owners cleaned and repaired the apartment and rented it out again. The case against the husband moved fairly quickly through the legal system, and thus my official involvement with it ended. As time went on, my recollections of the case faded and blended into the memories of all the other horrible things I have seen, although I still can't hear "Sweet Surrender" and not think of a young life cut way too short.

It was all over, or so I thought. It just so happened that our friend from chapter one, Deputy Mike, got dispatched to a call at that same apartment. Having been one of the first responders to the homicide, Mike had his own flood of emotions when he saw the familiar address pop up on his laptop screen. When Mike made contact with the current tenant his thoughts were on the former tenant, but he had a job to do. This time he was being called there for a much less weighty matter. The people had wanted to talk to an officer to see what could be done about the excessive noise coming from the upstairs neighbors, who partied all night—a common problem in large apartment complexes.

Mike wrote up what is called a "noise complaint," advised the people on their options for a little while, and then prepared to leave. As he made for the door, the woman stopped him.

"Ummm . . . sorry. This may seem like a silly question," she said tentatively, "but did something bad happen in these apartments?"

Mike felt the blood drain from his face as he cautiously responded, "Yeah."

"What happened?" she returned.

"Someone was murdered."

"Which unit?" inquired the woman.

"Are you sure you want to know?" Mike asked, the hair rising on the back of his neck.

"Yeah."

"This one," Mike replied, not knowing what to expect from the woman.

"Oh . . . okay. That makes sense," she said, completely satisfied by his answer. For her, the matter was now closed.

For Deputy Mike, however, it was not. Having been not a little disconcerted by her line of questioning, he had to know why she had brought it up.

Trying to sound as nonchalant as possible, Mike asked, "Why do you ask, ma'am?"

"Oh, it's nothing really," she replied, still sounding unconcerned. "It's just . . . sometimes the bathroom door will open by itself and the light will flick on. I figured it was something like that."

Deputy Mike did not know what to say. How had this woman, who ostensibly had no knowledge of the crime, been able to essentially pinpoint where the victim had died? Walking back to his patrol car, Mike was certainly pondering that particular question.

One thing seems clear: the echoes of this heinous crime lingered long after the CD player was turned off and the music faded.

Chapter Eighteen
Hard Hat

I realize that the following statement is a tad cliché, but it is nevertheless true that law enforcement agencies have a love/hate relationship with the media. On the one hand, the media can be very useful to law enforcement's cause. Certainly there is no better way to get the word out to the public about a suspect that needs to be located or an imminent public safety concern than to have such issues splashed across television and newspapers. Many a dangerous offender has been apprehended thanks to an alert citizen who saw or read about said person in the media.

On the other hand, the media does tend to sensationalize things, hence the axiom in journalism, "If it bleeds, it leads." As a result, stories are often presented in a very simplistic manner. There is a clear victim and a well-defined villain, an obvious right and apparent wrong. Many of the nuances that represent the reality of a given situation are stripped away, making complex events easily misinterpreted by the public at large.

Reporters also do not seem that preoccupied with the accuracy of quotes. While I was studying forensic science at Weber State University, one of my professors often said that in all the decades he had been in law enforcement, he had never been quoted correctly in the media. I have seen this to a lesser extent myself. In the handful of times some of my courtroom testimony has been quoted in the paper, the reporter seemed to paraphrase and interpret my words rather than quote me.

By and large our local print and television journalists have a job to do like the rest of us and are good to work with—and are even fun to tease. As a general rule, television folks take themselves less seriously than purveyors of print do, which reminds me of a curious incident that happened about a decade ago.

During this time, the downtown area of my fair city of Ogden was undergoing extensive renovation and revitalization. Old buildings were being fixed up. New buildings were going up, and it was to one of these new buildings that my buddy Jason and I got called one rainy spring morning. You see, there had been a terrible accident. One of the construction workers had fallen to his death from a very high perch, and CSI was called to investigate. After arriving at the construction site, we got out of our cars and looked around for the officer who had us dispatched to the scene. It did not take us long to find him, standing just outside the uncompleted building. The patrol officer in question was named John.

John is an unusual officer, in that he does not display a "Type A" personality as many officers do. Rather, John comes across as about the most easygoing guy you have ever met. Furthermore, he possesses what I would call a slow-burning intelligence. He is a man of few words and does not say much, but when he does, it is always good.

Unfortunately, not long after we found John someone else found him, too. As he was about to give Jason and me the details of the case and outline what he needed us to do, a reporter for our local newspaper walked right up to our little conference, pen in hand, ready to document this sad event for the reading public. He was a young fellow, and looked like he was just out of journalism school.

Then commenced a version of a stand-off one might see in a spaghetti western. The reporter looked at us expectantly, we crime scene investigators looked at the patrol officer waiting for him to say something, and Officer John weighed his options. Finally, John motioned for Jason and me to follow him deeper into the construction site—in fact, right to the building itself.

We complied, and when the intrepid reporter began to trail after us, John turned to him and told him that he could not follow. Upon hearing this the reporter underwent a visible change. All of a sudden his spine straightened, his chest puffed out, and a look of defiance etched itself on his youthful face. With squared jaw he asked, "Why not?"

To me, he looked ready and waiting to eviscerate any feeble reply from the lowly officer with a brilliantly delivered "freedom of the press" argument he learned from one of his journalism professors. In fact, he looked like he relished this opportunity to use his prepared speech; perhaps it was the first time he had the chance to do so.

He was not ready for John's response. Without missing a beat, John pointed at his head and said flatly, "You don't have a hard hat."

Right before my eyes this reporter's back slumped. A look of abject defeat replaced his haughty glare and he turned and departed without another word. It was the most amazing on-time response I had ever heard. It is something I would have thought of three hours later and then wished I would have said. It did not seem to matter that we ourselves were not wearing hard hats; John's brilliance was just something no journalism professor had, or could have prepared this poor lad for. In retrospect, it was not even fair.

I am a whole-hearted supporter of a free press and its role in a free and open society, yet this reporter could get his story without the show-and-tell at the actual spot where a man died, and without hearing all the gruesome details of the case. Come on—give the victim and their family their dignity, please. They deserve that much.

After praising John for his genius, we went on to do our CSI thing and photographically document the scene of this tragic death. Then it was on to the next horrible thing, and the next, and eventually the incident faded from my mind—that is, until a year or so later, when the building was finished, occupied, and I began to frequent one of the businesses that had sprung up in the new construction. My family and I were such regulars at this business that we became friends with one of the managers.

One day our manager friend mentioned in passing that their women's restroom was prone to strange goings-on. As I digested this revelation, I realized that the room in question was virtually on top of the death scene. Knowing of this spot's sad history, I naturally wondered if whatever was going on was the work of the restless spirit of the poor construction worker. I asked for details and my friend provided them. The anecdotes he offered were nothing earth-shattering: we were not talking the Amityville horror here. There was just a self-opening door here, a blinking light there; a radio with a mind of its own one day, and strange noises the other. None of the workers were that freaked out, but the anomalies were noted. Nevertheless, as I listened, memories of that rainy spring day flooded back to my mind and I could not help but wonder if the ghost who was haunting the women's bathroom was wearing his hard hat.

Chapter Nineteen
A Return Visit

People working in law enforcement have a lot of baggage. This can be physical, mental, or spiritual baggage, or often a combination of all three. One of the funny quirks that I have noticed in my own life is that I have way too much information about too many of the places in the town in which I live and work.

When I was younger in my career, I would drive around town running errands with my wife, and I would constantly be making comments that went something like this: "Someone got stabbed the other night in that green house on the corner," or, "That restaurant over there was burglarized yesterday. You should have seen how filthy the kitchen was. We are never eating there again;" or, "I had a call in those apartments last week. The people had marijuana growing in their bathroom."

You get the picture: way too much information. I do not often make such comments anymore, because my wife got a bit sick of it, and frankly, so did I. Oh, I may still think about the places I have been and the things I have seen, but it is just not worth the effort to mention it anymore.

Most of the time now, once a call is in the books, I really do not think about it again unless it is going to court. The one big exception are death scenes. With my obvious interest in the paranormal, and as I have collected more and more stories, I can't help but wonder if the crime scene where I have just spent so much time is going to end up haunted.

The trouble is, I can't rightly go back later to a former crime scene in the capacity of a crime scene investigator and ask the residents if their home is haunted. That would not be professional at all. I also can't simply show up on the front step of a place as a civilian. Imagine how that conversation would go: "Hi. I was here the other day taking pictures of your dead grandmother and have returned to find out if the old girl is still hanging around." My sheriff would be getting a call from an irate constituent in no time flat. I would be in hot water, off duty or not.

The vast majority of the time one is left to wonder about any new ghostly residents of this plane of existence. There are times when fate intervenes and you do get the information you want, even if, as in this case, you did not even know you were looking for it.

A story was related to me about a young single mother named Katie who moved into a very large apartment complex with her seven-year-old daughter and her dog, a red heeler/lab mix. Things were going along fine, and they were all adjusting to the new surroundings until one night about two months after they had moved in. Something woke mom up in the middle of the night. It felt like someone was shaking and tugging on her leg. As she opened her eyes, she saw something that made her blood run cold.

You see this mother, as many parents of young children do, slept with her door open and the hall light on just in case her daughter should wake in the night and require assistance. This time Katie did not see a child in need of a drink of water, but rather the silhouette of a man. Although she could not make out any features of his face, Katie could tell that the man was large and completely bald.

In her sleep-addled mind, Katie's first thought was that someone had broken into her house and meant her and her daughter harm. Flooded with panic, she began to scream bloody murder. Her large dog jumped up on the bed, glared at the doorway, and began to growl ferociously. Finally, Katie made a lunge for her bedside lamp and managed with trembling hands to click it on. Not knowing what to expect next, Katie certainly did not expect nothing, which is exactly what she got. No one was standing in the doorway! After collecting herself for a moment, she jumped up and rushed to her daughter's room. There was no intruder there, only her daughter sleeping soundly. A quick check of the rest of the apartment yielded no evidence of a break-in. The doors and windows were all still locked and intact, and none of her property was missing or disturbed.

As Katie went back to bed she had trouble falling asleep. Had there actually been a large, bald man standing in her doorway, or was it all simply a dream?

The dream scenario would be the most logical explanation had it not been for the reaction of her dog. He had acted as if he also had seen someone or something standing in the door. Katie was eventually able to fall asleep, and in the days to come, she tried to put the whole thing behind her.

The trouble was, she kept seeing someone standing in her bedroom door. It usually happened that she saw him out of the corner of her eye while watching television. She would quickly turn her head and nothing would be there. The nighttime visits even occurred occasionally.

It is human nature to grow accustomed to a recurring event, even if it is a strange one, and so it was with Katie, until something happened that upped the ante and changed the whole game.

One day, Katie's daughter was playing quietly with a toy phone. It is important to note this toy phone did not possess any electronic components, and therefore did not make any sounds, nor interact with its user; it just looked like a telephone.

Seizing upon this moment of domestic calm, Katie decided to grab a quick bath. As she lay there, relaxing in the warm water, she, like all good mothers, kept one ear on her daughter. She could clearly hear her playing through the open bathroom door. Katie's daughter was having a conversation with an imaginary friend on the toy phone.

Katie was only half listening when she heard her daughter ask the "person" on the other line if they wanted to be put on speakerphone so they could talk to her pet rat. What happened next brought Katie right out of the water. As clear and loud as can be, she heard a male voice respond to her daughter's inquiry by saying simply, "Hello?"

Katie grabbed a towel and ran to where her daughter was playing. She checked the television: it was off. She checked the radio: nothing. She asked her daughter if she had heard a man talking. The child said that she had not.

That was enough for Katie. She grabbed a few things for her and her daughter and moved in with family that very day. I guess seeing strange things was easier to live with than hearing strange things. The voice had not been particularly harsh or evil sounding, but it scared the living daylights out of her. The fact that her daughter had not heard it only made the situation worse.

Still having several months left on her lease, Katie weighed her options. She really did not want to go back to the apartment, but breaking the lease meant a rather hefty financial penalty. While she decided what to do Katie did some checking around. It turned out that a few years earlier, a man had taken his own life in the apartment below hers by placing a shotgun in his mouth. I know from many years on the job how violent and bloody such an end is.

Was the unwelcome guest in Katie's apartment the unfortunate man who had met such a gruesome end so close by? I suppose no one will ever really know for sure, but this haunting definitely fits the age-old pattern. No positive identification would be possible; Katie had never been able to clearly see the man's face. Under the circumstances, that was probably for the better.

Whatever the case, Katie did not go back for any length of time until three months had passed and the sound of that voice had faded in her ears. When she finally did, she regretted the decision. You see, she once again woke up in the middle of the night to find herself being watched from the doorway. This time, when she reached out for her lamp, her legs got tangled in the blanket and she fell on the floor and fractured her wrist.

Lease or no lease, Katie moved all of her belongings out and never returned.

Chapter Twenty
The Number of the Beast

As a man of science and law, I should not admit that I am a touch superstitious, but what the heck, I am, and so are most people in law enforcement. Most cops have their favorite gun or a particular way they load their gun. Forensic people also have their little quirks. My particular superstition revolves around my on-call night. I am convinced that if I go to bed on my on-call night without socks I will get called out for sure. Of course this is ridiculous, and of course I have been called out of bed many times with my feet shod, but I still do it, and I feel anxious if I do not. As it turns out, other members of my crew also have on-call rituals performed to ward off that four-thirty a.m. vehicle burglary call.

A crime scene investigator's superstitions might range beyond little rituals. A co-worker of mine swears she was cursed after she had to drive a hearse that was parked in our auto storage lot: her next four calls were all death investigations. To be fair to her, if you look at the frequency of calls we go on, four dead bodies in a row is a bit of a statistical anomaly.

When you look at the plethora of superstitions out there, numbers are something about which people can have strong feelings. They have their lucky numbers and their unlucky numbers. If you do not believe this just ask anyone who plays the lottery. Folks might also subscribe to astrology or numerology, where it is believed birthdates and other notable dates play a key role in one's very destiny.

There is one number that strikes dread in the hearts of people all over the western world: 666. This dread comes from a reading of the Book of Revelation in the New Testament. Chapter thirteen, verses seventeen and eighteen of Revelation, say:

And that no man might buy or sell, save he that had the mark, or the name of the beast, or the number of his name.

Here is wisdom. Let him that hath understanding count the number of the beast: for it is the number of a man; and his number is Six hundred threescore and six.

For thousands of years these words and this number have fascinated people due to its apparent association with the devil and its portent of evil things to come. Consequently, this number has ingrained itself in the public psyche and makes frequent appearances in popular culture. For instance, the British heavy metal group Iron Maiden composed a little ditty entitled "The Number of the Beast," which is an epic example of '80s hair metal.

As it turns out, law enforcement personnel swim in a veritable sea of numbers. Every day one deals constantly with addresses, case numbers, evidence numbers, marker numbers, birthdates, license plate numbers, and so on.

Whenever during the course of your duties you get a case number, or an address, or a score on the fingerprint computer that is or that contains somehow this feared of all numbers 666, there are invariable comments made and a sense of foreboding felt, as irrational as it may be.

This brings us to a lovely day a few autumns ago. I got a call to respond to a death investigation at a certain address about a block away from my favorite 7-Eleven. When I got to the scene, I instantly saw that this was no normal death call. Usually people who die of natural causes outside of a medical facility die inside their own homes. This poor old gal had simply passed on to the next life right there on the sidewalk, clutching a bag of recently purchased goodies from 7-Eleven.

There were no signs of foul play, and an officer responded to the convenience store and talked to the clerks. They remembered her in there just a short time before and recalled that she did not look very good, being pale and breathing heavily. That would tend to indicate some health problems, but there was no outward sign of what had killed this lady. Simply put, we had no idea why this lady was dead on the sidewalk.

I thoroughly photographed the scene and the deceased, and the deputy medical examiner inspected the body. When we were ready to move her, the 7-Eleven bag was pried from her hand and the contents examined. To make sure everything fit together, the receipt was scrutinized to see if the time-of-purchase matched the general time frame the gals at the 7-Eleven had given us. It all matched and the receipt was set aside.

It was not until the deceased was taken away and I was about to leave that I casually picked up the receipt and looked at it again. I do not remember why; I just did. This time it was not the time-of-purchase that stuck out to me, but the cost of the items in the bag. The total, with tax, of the last purchase ever made by this woman who died of unknown causes on the sidewalk was six dollars and sixty-six cents.

Chapter Twenty-One
The Unwinnable Fight

A young intern rode along with me one day, who, unlike legions of her "CSI"-watching generation, was not interested in forensic science, but rather wanted to be a cop. I was not at all insulted by this state of affairs, but was frankly relieved. Instead of spending my shift unraveling Hollywood's mistakes and exaggerations, I got the opportunity to listen for a change. I listened to her hopes, dreams, and plans and felt no obligation to offer any guidance, since patrol work is not my end of the shop.

As the day went on, we had a call with a patrol officer for whom I have a great deal of respect. This officer, who has a story in this book, is not only tough and resourceful, but also a bit of a thinker. He, unlike many of his comrades, has the ability to momentarily step out of his shoes and objectively examine what is going on around him. This ability gives him some valuable insights regarding not only a given situation he might encounter during a shift, but also the law enforcement profession as a whole. It was exactly these kinds of insights that my intern was eager to hear.

I introduced my ride-along to the sage officer, gave him a brief explanation of her career goals, and then set to work processing the scene of a vehicle burglary. As this seasoned veteran candidly discussed the realities of patrol work, he expressed to her what he felt was one of the most peculiar aspects of his job. As he put it, "When a normal person hears gun fire, they run away from it. We run toward it. Unlike normal people, we cannot shun a fight. Being a cop definitely requires a certain kind of person."

While this admonition hopefully helped my intern soberly evaluate her occupational goals, a story I heard at a later time left me thinking that there are some fights best left not fought. This story revolves around a police officer, his wife, and a new condominium.

An officer named Damian and his wife were excited when they moved into a brand new condo in Ogden, Utah. As time went on, they began to notice that all was not right with their new residence. From time to time the most horrible smell would suddenly show up. It smelled like a broken freezer full of rotting meat one time and repulsive feces the next. The smell always seemed to originate from a certain corner of the front room. Damian and his wife would try and identify the source of the reek, but were never able to find a cause. As suddenly as the smell appeared it would disappear, only to return later.

Then there were times when the television would change channels by itself. Damian would fall asleep watching ESPN with the volume set low and wake up to *Headbangers Ball* on MTV with the sound cranked. The heavy, loud, and as he put it "satanic" sounding music would shock him awake and leave his heart pounding. But that was nothing compared to the dreams he started to have.

On several occasions he dreamt that a grim reaper was in his room, hovering at the side of his bed. One night things got a little too real for Damian when the reaper not only watched him but reached out and grabbed his arm. The skeletal hand of the entity felt so real to Damian that he jumped out of bed screaming for Jesus to protect him.

The strangeness went to another level when Damian's three-year-old niece came to visit one day. When the child walked into the front room she stopped and noticeably cringed when the corner so inexorably linked to the periodic awful smells came into view. After staring at the empty corner for a moment she pointed to it and said, "There's a bad man there!"

Damian, assuming that this utterance was the result of the overactive imagination of a child, wanted to play along with his niece. He walked over to the corner, said, "Oh . . . there's a bad man there, huh? I'll show him!" and with that he began to punch, swing, and jab at an unseen figure standing where the girl had indicated. Being a fun and playful uncle, and a having a good relationship with the child, Damian expected the girl to laugh and cheer as he pretended to beat up the "bad man," but he did not get the reaction he expected. Instead of mirth, he got terror. Upon seeing her uncle punch at the air, the small child lay on the floor, curled up in the fetal position, and screamed, "No! No! Stop!" repeatedly until Damian ceased his imaginary fight. Of all the strange things that had happened to them up to this point, this was the most disconcerting. A terrorized three-year-old is something not easily dismissed.

Life has a way of moving on, and the episode involving the "bad man" was quickly in the rearview mirror. Soon, the excitement surrounding an impending camping trip replaced their unease. With only days to go before their departure, Damian placed his phone on the corner of the loveseat near the dreaded corner of the front room and ran upstairs for just a minute. When he came back down his phone was nowhere to be seen. Perplexed, Damian looked around the loveseat. The phone was not on the floor. He pulled up the cushions and looked in the nooks and crannies; still no phone. He asked his wife. She had not touched it. They called his phone with another phone. Not a sound was heard. The doors and windows of the condo were all locked, so he ruled out theft. The phone had simply vanished into thin air.

The night before they were to leave Damian and his wife had some last minute shopping to do, so they headed for a local big box store. Once there, Damian waited in the car as his wife ran in to pick up the needed items. When she got back to the car, she loaded her purchases into the vehicle and then asked, "Oh, so you found your phone?"

"No," he replied. "I haven't seen it for days. Why?"

"Huh . . . " she started nervously. "When I was in the store, my phone rang. It was buried in my purse so I couldn't get to it in time. When I checked it, I saw that it was your phone that had called!"

This odd turn of events prompted Damian to call his mobile carrier and check if there had been other activity on the phone since it had gone missing. Maybe someone had stolen it after all and was running around town racking up a huge phone bill. When the company checked the phone's activity, they found that there had only been one call made in the last few days. It was the missed call to his wife's cell phone.

They never did find that phone, even when they eventually moved away from the condo and removed all their furniture. The story of the missing cell phone certainly leaves Damian with two questions: where did the phone go, and who used it to call his wife? To this day neither question has a satisfactory answer. Such voids of facts often lead to speculation—and speculate I will. Could it be that the "bad man," whomever it was, called Damian for a rematch?

Chapter Twenty-Two
A Last Goodbye

When I was a student at Weber State University, I asked one of my professors how he had emotionally coped with the horrible things he had witnessed over the years. My professor told me that his attitude had always been that the victims of the crimes he was investigating did not need nor want another person crying for them. They wanted justice. He was in a position to help provide justice, and that was what he focused on, rather than the tragedy before him.

I took this advice to heart, and over the span of my own career it has provided some measure of emotional insulation against the horror I have routinely witnessed. Unfortunately, this coping mechanism goes right out the window when it comes to kids.

Crimes perpetrated against children are by far the hardest situations to deal with emotionally for an investigator. Even crimes where kids are only secondary participants or witnesses can take a psychological toll on law enforcement workers, mainly because it negates a fundamental coping mechanism utilized by people working in the business.

When you deal with an adult victim of a crime, it is easy to tell yourself that the person's actions or choices caused, or at least increased the likelihood of, their victimization. This is not always true or justified, but it is a strategy that is sometimes used to mitigate emotional stress.

There is naturally a continuum or a sliding scale at play here. If you work a case where a gang member, wanted for several murders is killed by a rival, this approach works quite well. If you are pointing your camera at a young single mother who was driving home from the night shift when she was struck and killed by a drunk driver, you do not find much to make yourself feel better.

I know this tactic of "victimization rationalization" sounds horrible to the average person, but if you bleed for every person whose blood you photograph, you do not last long in this business; you quickly burn out and have to "hang it up." One needs something to help dull the pain, and this works as well as anything—except when it comes to kids. It is impossible to think that a child shares any blame whatsoever in the bad things that happen to or around them; it just does not work on any level.

That is why cases where kids are involved stay with you for a long time, if not forever. You can never un-see them.

I will never forget the face of one particular ten-year-old boy. I was called to his house because his mother had been caught in a domestic violence situation. She was the aggressor. My job was to photograph injuries sustained by the combatants. Kids are usually very interested in what we are doing, and this little guy was no different. He watched me very carefully.

Things were going along fine until I finished my work. The cop slapped the cuffs on his mom and started to read her rights. When the boy realized what was going on, the expression on his faced flashed from shock to fear, then to disgust and hatred for the people depriving him of his mother. It did not matter to him that I had no say in whether his mother was arrested or not, or that I was simply there to document facts. I was not spared his anger. I was just another part of the apparatus breaking up his family. Like I said, it is a face I will never forget.

The combination of kids and crime make for heartrending situations all the way around. Imagine the apprehension a certain investigator felt as he was about to interview a kindergarten-age girl who did not know yet that her mother had been murdered the night before. With a pit in his stomach, the detective watched this young child playing with her toys, unaware that the monthly visit with her mother which had occurred a few days prior would be the last time she would ever see her in this life.

To tell the whole story we have to back up a bit. A woman in her thirties had been stabbed to death in her apartment. She was found by friends after she had not shown up for work. CSI and detectives were notified. We responded and began to process the scene, looking for evidence. That first night of the investigation there were no strong suspects in the case. As detectives tried to piece together whom this victim was and what her recent activities were, they discovered that the unfortunate woman had two children. They were also able to ascertain that her kids had spent the previous weekend with her on a scheduled visit. Detectives wanted to talk to the children to determine if the mother had been acting strangely, or if the kids had seen or heard mention of anyone bothering their mother.

The tricky part was the fact that the detectives wanted to talk to the kids before they knew of their mother's passing. As heartless as this may sound, there is a certain logic in this course of action: nothing is more devastating to a child than finding out that one of their parents has died, let alone that they were murdered. The investigators wanted to glean any potentially crucial information the children might have before they were overcome with grief.

So it was that our detective, Shane, found himself in a room with the two children and their father and aunt. The adults were aware of the fate of the mother. The children were not. The kids played for a while; Shane held back, letting them get used to his presence. After a little while, the aunt announced to the children that Shane had a few questions for them about their mother.

At the mention of her mother, the five-year-old perked right up and made an announcement that sent chills running down Shane's spine.

"Mommy came and saw me last night," she said cheerfully.

"She did?" asked the confused aunt, knowing full well that was impossible.

"Oh, yes," affirmed the child. "I was sleeping and she woke me up. She told me that she would be going away for a while, but not to worry about her because she was fine."

After this pronouncement none of the adults in the room knew what to say. How does one respond to that? Shane awkwardly asked the questions he had come to ask and then left, leaving the difficult task of death notification to the family. Eventually, through the tireless efforts of Shane and the other detectives, not to mention some nifty forensic science work, the case was solved and the perpetrator now resides at the Utah State Penitentiary.

The matter is not over for Shane. All these years later, he still thinks about the girl, ponders his conversation with her, and wonders if the girl simply dreamt that her mother had paid her a visit, or is the power of a mother's love even stronger than death?

Chapter Twenty-Three
Who's Haunting Our Lab?

In my forensic science classes at Weber State University, I was taught a principle of problem-solving known as "Ockham's Razor." Named after its creator, William of Ockham (c.1287–1347), this principle states that the correct solution to a problem is more often than not the simplest one. Ockham's Razor is not the province of forensic scientists, but is used in all avenues of science and philosophy, and has hopefully been keeping us all on track for a long time.

"Keeping it simple" is especially important while processing the scenes of homicides. If one is not careful, the fertile imaginations of those involved can easily lead an investigation far afield. As mentioned in an earlier chapter, "who-done-its" are rare. You usually know the person who killed you. A lover's quarrel is much more likely to lead to your death than a team of highly trained ninja monkeys practicing for their next big hit. It is just the way it is.

Not every investigator is a practitioner of Ockham's Razor. When I was a rookie, there was this detective who used to crack the crime scene investigation team up. To him, every person died in a manner befitting a *Tom and Jerry* cartoon. This guy conjured up scenarios as farfetched as bowling balls rolling down rain gutters on to ironing boards, which in turn flipped anvils on to people's heads. It was crazy. My old boss and mentor, Russ Dean, was then compelled to disprove this detective's latest wild theory through careful inductive reasoning, at which point the detective slunk away until the next time. The vast majority of the time the simplest solution is the correct one.

What if there is no simple, logical answer to a question? What then? Here we are in a book of ghost stories discussing principles of logic and reasoning. There will be those who say these two topics do not belong together at all.

Even though the pages of science and philosophy textbooks do not devote much ink to the esoteric, the world of the supernatural does have its own kind of logic.

As a basic example, let us say a person dies a gruesome death in a certain place. At a later time people report that place is now haunted. Using a paranormal version of cause and effect, the conclusion may be drawn that the person who died horribly in that place is now haunting it.

Such a conclusion is the simplest, but what if even those rules break down? What if the person said to be haunting a place is, as of the writing of this book, still alive? What if the ghost bothering people while they are trying to work is . . . me?

Did I lose you? Well, I am pretty lost, too. I do not know what to make of all this, but here we go. One night, a co-worker of mine was working the late shift alone. No one else was in the office; this point must be very clear.

At about two a.m., she found herself in the records room, next to our evidence room in the back corner of our facility. With her back to the door she filed her completed casework. While she was thus engaged, she heard a voice call out her name, "Angie?" She was startled by the voice, but not frightened. Why should she be? After all, she recognized the voice; it was mine. She turned around, expecting to see me in the doorway, where the sound had emanated from. I was not in the doorway. No one was in the doorway.

She called out my name and began to search the office for me. Surely it had been me. How could she fail to recognize the voice of her trainer? She found no one. The office was empty, as it had been before. There was no sign of anyone having been there other than herself. The main door to our office makes a loud clanking noise when it shuts because the magnetic lock snaps the door shut. Angie had not heard that telltale sound.

At this point Angie became extremely frightened and had to leave the office for the rest of the night. She called me in the morning just to double check that I had not been there. I had not.

I did not put much stock in this story. Our building is an exceedingly noisy place. The metal roof creaks and groans with the heating and cooling of the day. Various machinery kicks on and off at all hours. Also, anyone who has worked nights knows that sleep deprivation can do funny things to your mind. Angie had just thought she heard my voice, right? Well, such rationalizations might have worked . . . if it had not happened again to a different co-worker.

Months later, Shanae was working in the lab, processing some evidence and looking for latent fingerprints. The records and evidence rooms are situated off the lab, so Shanae was close to the scene of Angie's "encounter." She was utterly alone in the office as was Angie, but this time my colleague was working during the day, not the bitter watches of the night.

As she plugged away on her casework, she was surprised to hear my voice call her name from the front office area loud and clear. The fact that she heard my voice was not what surprised her. It was not out of the ordinary for people to swing by the office for this reason or that, even if they were not working. What surprised her was the fact that she had not heard the clank of the front door. Nevertheless, she called out a happy greeting in return to "my" greeting. The trouble was, no answer came in reply. She left the lab to see where I had gone and why I had not responded to her greeting. After a quick scan of the office she found that she was quite alone. No cars were parked in front of our building and there was no sign of anyone having been there.

We humans seem to get less freaked out in the daylight than we do at night, so Shanae did not flee the office as Angie had done, but she was certainly perplexed and agitated.

It is easy to dismiss one weird story; it is harder, although still possible, to dismiss another similar tale. But what about a third? This one may be the weirdest yet.

For the sake of context, I have a very distinctive sneeze. I get it from my father, actually. He sneezed in a particular way, and I somehow picked it up. Think long wind-up and short but loud delivery. Anyone who knows me well will recognize my sneeze. The reason I am sharing this tidbit of personal information with you is that one day another co-worker was working alone in the office. As she sat in her office, she heard me sneeze. Like I said, if you know me well, you recognize my sneeze. As with the other two co-workers Nalleli was surprised, because she had not heard the clank of the door that heralds someone's arrival to the office.

To her great credit and the credit of her upbringing, her astonishment did not make her lose her manners. She politely called out, "God bless you." There was no answer. She got up from her chair and left her office to see why I had not responded to such a courteous gesture on her part. No one was there. She was very much alone in the office.

I really do not know what to make of these stories. Is it possible to haunt a place before you are dead? Were those spiritual encounters, or rather some slice of time—an echo, if you will—captured and somehow replayed? Did my co-workers have a mental breakdown due to the chronic stress associated with a career in law enforcement? As true as that last statement eventually will be for all of us, I do not think there is a simple answer. In this instance Ockham's razor has gone dull.

Chapter Twenty-Four
A Face at My Window

Of all the changes in law enforcement I have witnessed over the years, the increased number of women entering the professions is one of the most positive. Some view the fact that female officers are not generally as large or aggressive as their male counterparts as a negative thing. I take the opposite stance. A patrol officer encounters a wide array of situations during any given shift. Some situations require a hammer. Some situations require a feather. You need cops who can bust a few heads when needed. You also need cops who know how to ratchet down tense situations. Because female officers do not typically rely on their fists to resolve things, they are master de-escalators.

Case in point: a few years back, I was working one late night, heading back to my office after a call. The back road to our facility is a fairly less-traveled lane, especially at night. I turned on to this street and was surprised to see a man standing smack dab in the middle of it. To add to my astonishment, he was frantically waving his arms at me with a wild look in his eyes. Bear in mind that I am just a geeky crime scene guy. I am not a first responder, I am on the cleanup crew! I am in an official looking vehicle, so I felt obligated to stop and see if this man needed help.

As soon as I stopped my vehicle and rolled down the window, he ran right up to me and started to yell and scream in my face that someone was trying to shoot him. I tried to assure him that he was safe now, while inside hoping some stray bullet that was meant for my new friend would not instead find me. My assurances did nothing to quell this man's anxiety. In fact, he became more agitated and tried to open my car door. At this point I began to suspect that this man was not a target for assassination, but rather mentally disturbed or on drugs. It was time to call in some professional help. I grabbed my police radio and broadcasted my location and situation. I asked, probably with a tremor in my voice, for some assistance from officers more equipped to handle such situations. This radio traffic seemed only to amp this poor fellow up even more, and before I knew it he was trying to crawl through my window. When I told my co-workers this story they all asked, "Why didn't you simply drive away?"

"Oh yes," I responded, "I can just see the headlines now . . . 'Heartless CSI Drags Local Man to Death!'"

Anyway, for what seemed like an eternity the guy was yelling and trying to climb into my car, and I was hollering at him and trying to push him out. Finally the first officer arrived. It was a deputy sheriff named Stephanie. We all simply call her Steph. Even though my little dust-up was not occurring in her area, she heard my plea for help and high-tailed it to my location, doubtless driving faster than she would like to admit to her supervisors. Needless to say, I was greatly relieved at her arrival. Then, in what I can only describe as a miraculous feat, she had the guy out of my car, sitting on the ground in handcuffs, and calm as can be in no time flat. I was astounded. She had the fellow virtually eating out of her hand and all she used were her words and her calm and assertive manner.

As it turned out, this man was having a mental breakdown and had been running all over town pounding on people's doors and trying to force his way inside. It is fortunate that a frightened homeowner had not shot him. Steph may very well have saved his life. I certainly never forgot that night, especially since something similar happened to me a few years later.

I was once again on that same road, this time trying to make my way home after a long night. The trouble was, I could not make it home quite yet because a train was blocking my path. As I sat and waited on the dark and lonely street I pulled out my phone and began to look at the internet. There are no street lights on this stretch of road, and the only light at hand was coming from my headlights and an occasional flicker from passing railcars.

Suddenly something made me involuntarily whip my head toward my window. What greeted me made my heart skip a beat. Glaring at me through the closed window was a wizened, bearded old man. He did not look angry or frightened, but rather wore a blank look on his face. The funny thing was, I had not seen him anywhere near the train tracks when I had pulled up, and the area was pretty open. I had no explanation for his sudden appearance other than the possibility that the darkness had hidden him. With the above mentioned encounter on that very same street still fresh in my mind, this time I decided against rolling my window down. After all, I was not sure if Steph was around to save me this time.

"What do you want?" I shouted through the glass after I had composed myself.

"Where am I?" the man yelled back.

"What do you mean, 'where are you?'" I asked incredulously.

"I was dropped off here. I don't know where I am," returned the man vacantly.

"This is seventeenth street." I responded.

"East or west?" he asked.

By this time the train had passed and I was more than ready to end this encounter and head home.

"West," I replied. The man nodded and seemed satisfied.

As I popped my vehicle into gear and pulled away I let out a nervous laugh. "What is it about me on this street?" I wondered. Immediately I glanced up into my rearview mirror to take one last look at the fellow who had given me such a start. The trouble was I couldn't; he was gone.

Chapter Twenty-Five
The Restless Mate

One of the more common questions I get asked when people find what I do is whether the horrible things I see give me nightmares. That is certainly a valid question, and folks are usually surprised when I say generally no. In all of my time in the business, I can think of only one work related dream that woke me up in a cold sweat.

In the dream, I had responded to a school-like place on a death investigation call. There was a deceased individual seated in one of those one-piece slide-in desks, his head resting on his arms, which were folded on the writing surface. In the room with me was another person, probably the officer who had called me. I approached the corpse and looked through the viewfinder of my camera in preparation of snapping a picture, a thing I have done hundreds if not a thousand times before. This time, as I got close to the body, the eyes popped open and he began to get up from the desk. The other person in the room with me started to scream and I woke up with my heart pounding. It is probably a good thing I do not dream about work that often.

I have asked my colleagues over the years about their work dreaming habits and their responses vary. Some people dream about work all the time and some, like myself, do so only rarely. But what about the spouses of crime scene investigators? Could it be that they might have nightmares about what they themselves have not experienced? Well, it appears that such was the case with the husband of a co-worker of mine—or was it something more?

Shanae's husband Thomas is usually a very sound sleeper. This is an important skill for the spouse of a person who comes and goes at all hours of the night. Usually he does not stir much at all. One night Shanae was jolted awake by Thomas thrashing about wildly in bed. He was whipping his arms to and fro and mumbling something incomprehensible. Shanae tried to wake and calm him, but to no avail. He kept muttering and writhing until all of a sudden he shouted out a name that sent chills up and down Shanae's spine. You see, the name her husband shouted out was the name of the victim on Shanae's latest homicide case. As shocked as she was, her husband's outburst seemed to soothe him and he fell back into a deep sleep. Unfortunately, the shock of hearing that name blurted so randomly into the night shook her up, and she did not join his blissful state for quite a while.

In the morning, still disturbed by the previous night's events, Shanae told her husband about what had happened and asked him if he remembered anything. After thinking for a second, he said that he did remember dreaming that this homicide victim was in their bedroom and that he had been trying to shoo her away. It was not until he yelled the person's name that she had departed. Shanae felt the blood drain from her face. Considering some of the eerie things that have occurred to her at our lab, she found herself wondering whether what Thomas had experienced was simply a dream. Then a chilling thought occurred to her.

"What was this person trying to do that made you so upset?" Shanae asked.

"At first, she was just standing at the foot of our bed. That was bad enough, but then she started walking," replied Thomas.

"Where?"

"Toward your side of the bed," Thomas responded slowly. "She was going for you."

Chapter Twenty-Six
What About the Guy Standing Next to You?

One common thing you hear from people you meet on the job, or from those who simply find out what you do, is "Oh, I couldn't do what you do." They usually go on to explain that they would not be able to handle some of the more gruesome aspects of the job.

Even people who work in other realms of law enforcement have said that to me. Specifically, I have had several corrections officers express to me that sentiment. The funny thing is that I feel the exact same way about their job.

You see, we get called to go inside our county jail all the time. Calls for service at a county jail range from a minor property damage call to a suicide or homicide. We respond to them all, and every time that big metal door slams shut and locks behind me, my heart sinks. I have just a tiny moment of panic where I think I will not be able to get out again. It probably does not help that the corrections officers like to tell you that it is understood that in case of prison riot any captured law enforcement personnel will not be negotiated for. Anyway, I just feel a little trapped and would not like to feel that way every day coming to work.

As it turns out, it is not only old, foolish crime scene investigators with active imaginations who feel trapped inside of jails, but also restless spirits. There are countless stories from all over the world regarding haunted prisons and jails old and new. Alcatraz Prison in San Francisco harbor is certainly among the most famous, but you do not have to be famous to have your fair share of paranormal activity. There is action right in our own local jails.

From the old county jail right here in town where I work, a story came to me. One of my corrections officer friends told me of a time when she stepped out from an office into a hall carrying a clipboard she needed for her nightly rounds. Suddenly and without warning the clipboard was snatched out of her hands by an unseen force and hurled down the hall. Perhaps you

105

might say that she just dropped it, or that it simply slipped out of her hands, but she felt the tug and vainly attempted to resist.

As a testament to my friend's fortitude, this brush with the unexplained did not cause her to fear her workplace, nor to avoid the subject of ghosts forevermore. On the contrary, she had a little fun with it. Many of the female inmates in a certain section of the jail swore up and down that a female ghost with long dark hair pulled over her face walked by their cells in the middle of the night. This apparition naturally freaked them all out. None of the officers had ever seen anything strange, and no one matching that description had ever died in that part of the jail; nevertheless, claims of visitation were not uncommon.

One night, my friend removed her hat, pulled her long, dark hair in front of her eyes, and slowly walked down the corridor, passing before the cell windows in this "haunted" section of the jail. In the ensuing uproar, this prankster could not contain her laughter for too long and the ruse was quickly discovered. Needless to say, she was not very popular with the inmates for a while after.

The eerie goings-on at our jail are tame compared to a jail in a neighboring county. According to the employee of that particular facility who related these accounts to me, ghostly phenomena are so common there they are expected. The sounds of footsteps echoing through empty halls and the racket of slamming doors are a regular occurrence in this facility. Two tales that this young lady recounted to me stick out above the others.

To understand this pair of stories better, you need to have a basic understanding of how many modern jails are built. To allow a minimum number of employees to observe and supervise the maximum number of inmates, many correctional facilities are built utilizing a "pod" structure.

There is a central command area with windows for walls resembling, and often referred to as, a large fish tank. Surrounding the fish tank on all sides are the large rooms containing a common area with tables and individual jail cells or bunks, depending on the level of security. In the central command area the wall facing it is also made of glass, a situation where the corrections officers can see the inmates when they are out of their cells and the inmates can see the corrections officers. Even when the inmates are in their cells they can see into central most of the time, although the officers can't see them. This allows the inmates some privacy. If the corrections officers need to see what is going on in a cell, they have to go into the pod and look through a small window in the cell door. The exercise yards also have a glass wall, allowing inmates to be observed when inside.

Another feature that modern jails have is a call button from each cell that allows inmates to communicate with the "fish tank" if they need something, and allows central to communicate with the inmates. As with most call buttons, there is usually a buzzer or some other indication that a button has been activated.

Bearing all this in mind, imagine, if you will, a young corrections clerk working late one night at a desk with an excellent view of the pod. As she plugged away at her paperwork, she absentmindedly looked up briefly from her stack of papers toward the glass wall of the exercise yard and then back down to what she was doing.

As anyone who has worked graveyard shifts can attest to, a sleep-deprived mind is not always the nimblest of instruments. Suddenly she popped her head back up and stared at the window. Had she just seen what she thought she had seen? No one was there. Of course no one was there; all the inmates were tucking into bed for the night. Nevertheless, she could have sworn she had seen a female inmate standing outside in the yard staring at her from the night. Something seemed not quite right with the prisoner: she looked pale, had disheveled hair, and seemed very angry. She was also wearing an inmate uniform that our clerk had never seen before.

Needless to say, my associate was very unnerved by what she had seen and kept glancing at the glass wall the rest of the night. She especially had a difficult time getting the hate-filled eyes of the woman out of her mind.

The next day, when our friend came in to work, she mentioned the occurrence to her co-workers. Upon hearing her tale one of her colleagues, who was the amateur historian of the jail, told her to hold her thought for a minute while he grabbed something. He returned with a scrapbook of sorts and thumbed through the book until he found what he was looking for. It was a picture of a female inmate—the same inmate who had stared through the glass wall the night before, wearing exactly the same outfit.

Our clerk exclaimed that it was whom she had seen the night before. "Who was she?" the clerk asked, "and why is she wearing those weird clothes?"

The armchair historian closed the book and looked gravely at our friend. "She is an inmate who hung herself in this jail years ago," he replied, "and those are the jumpsuits they wore back then."

It seems our corrections clerk can't get away from the paranormal, and in fact the story gets more disconcerting. One night she was working alone in the "fish tank." Let me reiterate that she was alone—quite alone.

At some point in the middle of the night an inmate buzzed the clerk from the inmate's cell. It is not uncommon for inmates to buzz central at all hours, especially the high-maintenance ones. What surprised her were the inmate's words over the intercom, "Will you stop bugging me?" he pleaded.

"What are you talking about?" she returned.

"Will you please stop pushing my call button?" he responded. "I'm trying to sleep."

Shocked by this accusation, she replied, "Believe me, I haven't been pushing your call button. Not even once."

The inmate uttered a response that she will never forget.

"What about the guy standing next to you?"

Final Evidence

When I started writing this book, my intent was to get on paper some of the fun stories I had heard while sucking down "Big Gulps" in the back of my favorite 7-Eleven or sitting around waiting for a search warrant to be signed. It was in no way, shape, or form meant to be a treatise on the paranormal—more as a collection of folklore. After all, one of the wonderful things about a career in law enforcement is the intense camaraderie and the storytelling culture that goes along with it. When officers and crime scene investigators hang it up after years on the force, they by and large, and despite all of the hardships, miss it—sometimes badly. They do not miss the midnight callouts. They do not miss the blood and guts. They do not miss the stress and tension. They miss friendships that can only be built in extraordinary circumstances, and they miss the stories told along the way. That is what I am trying to do here: celebrate those tales.

As I gathered these stories, I could not help but notice certain patterns. It stands to reason; I am in the business of examining evidence and following that evidence where it leads. It turns out not all ghost stories are created equal.

Some of the hauntings described in this text fit nicely into the category of the "restless spirit" belonging to a person who died a tragic or untimely death. The ghost who followed Mitch home is an excellent example of this paradigm.

Other tales adhere more closely to a "captured moment in time" archetype. Some paranormal researchers claim that ghostly encounters are simply a moment of time that has been captured—recorded, if you will—by the universe somehow and are replayed from time to time, much to the alarm of those who witness them. My ethereal sneeze certainly seems to be an example of this, as does the phantom history class at Weber State University. I do not know the complete history of the Social Science building, but if an entire history class, along with its professor, had died mid-lesson, giving rise to a "restless spirit" scenario, I am pretty sure I would have heard of it.

Another interesting trend I have noticed is that there seems to be a lot of paranormal activity surrounding evidence rooms and their associated labs. A lot of the strangeness that occurs in the Social Science Building at Weber State University happens on the second floor where the evidence room used to be. An agency I know of in Salt Lake valley has radios that turn on by themselves and random numbers that stream across the screens of calculators that are not being touched. In the lab of a friend in California, office chairs roll across carpeted floors from one side of the room to the other. I know California is prone to earthquakes, but nothing else in the lab is moving except for the chairs.

It is as if spirits are somehow attached to their former possessions or their bloody clothing drying in the forensic clothes dryer. They do not want to let go of the evidence we have collected.

It is fitting that this last chapter deal with evidence. The most common kind of evidence I collect on a daily basis is photographic evidence. It is said that a picture is worth a thousand words, and so it is. A photograph has a power few other things have. It accurately captures enormous amounts of detail, but also conveys emotion. People tend to believe what they see in photographs, especially when they have not been tampered with.

Certain kinds of cameras can even see that which is invisible to the naked eye, such as the infrared (IR) camera. In forensics, we use infrared to see blood or gunshot residue on dark surfaces, or for seeing through certain inks on a document with obliterated writing, or to make writing on charred documents visible.

One night I was assisting my co-worker Shanae on a shooting case. She had the clothing of an individual who had been shot spread out on a table in our lab and wanted me to photograph the clothing with the IR camera. This way we could search for gunshot residue in an attempt to ascertain which of the several holes in the garment was the entrance hole.

I pulled the IR camera out of the case and pointed it at Shanae. Behind her was the open door into our garage bay. We bring cars into this bay that require extensive processing. At the very moment I held the camera up and pushed the shutter release button two cars were parked inside; two cars in which people had recently been killed.

I looked at the LCD on the back of the camera to check my shot. The first thing that came to my attention was Shanae's smiling face. But then something else caught my eye: in the open doorway into our garage bay were four oval blobs. They had no business being there. There was no glare. There was no dust on the lens. I cannot account for what caused those blobs to appear in the picture, but they were there.

And so, at the end of a book that started out as a collection of law enforcement folklore and not as an attempt to prove that ghosts are real, have I done the opposite? Did I capture something with that infrared camera that proves life beyond the grave? You be the judge. A picture, after all, is worth a thousand words.

"THE END"

PAUL RIMMASCH graduated from Weber State University in Ogden, Utah, with a bachelor's degree in forensic science and a minor in photography. He has worked as a crime scene investigator for Weber-Metro CSI since 1997, and is a three-time recipient of the Weber County Sheriff's Office Medal of Merit. Paul has certifications through the International Association for Investigations in latent fingerprint examination and forensic photography. The author of previous works *The Lost Stones* and *The Lost Mine*, Paul has also published articles in *The Journal of Forensic Identification* and *Ancient American* magazine. He is an adjunct professor at Weber State University and is active in the training of police officers and crime scene investigators. Paul is a lifelong devotee of campfire stories.